The 'Reiki' Factor in
The Radiance Technique®
Expanded Edition

"Celebrating Your Radiance"

The 'Reiki' Factor in
The Radiance Technique®
Expanded Edition

Barbara Ray, Ph.D.

Radiance Associates   St. Petersburg, Florida

First Printing, January 1983
Second Printing, September 1983
Third Printing, May 1984
Fourth Printing, February 1985
Fifth Printing, June 1986
Sixth Printing, September 1988
Seventh Printing, November 1992

Expanded Edition

First Edition © 1983 by Dr. Barbara Ray
Second Edition © 1985 by Dr. Barbara Ray
Expanded Edition © 1988 by Dr. Barbara Ray
Expanded Edition © 1992 by Dr. Barbara Ray

Library of Congress Catalog Card Number 92-083725

ISBN 0-933267-06-1

Cover Artwork © 1988 by Dr. Barbara Ray

Printed in the United States of America

This book is dedicated to *you*, the reader–the seeker. May you find in it something for which you are searching in your journey.

A SPECIAL READER'S NOTE: Throughout this book you will notice that I sometimes use The Radiance Technique® which includes the correct ® delineating it as a registered service mark. This mark is registered for the use of The Radiance Technique Association International, Inc. and for Authorized Instructors. It denotes this authentic technique and no other. Its use in books such as this is to refer to the actual and authentic technique itself and no others. Sometimes in this book, I have used the words without the registered mark, which is correct to do since it has previously been introduced properly. I have also used TRT to stand for this service-marked phrase.

Contents

In selecting the title, *The 'Reiki' Factor in The Radiance Technique®*, I am referencing the *factor* of Universal, Transcendental, Radiant, Light Energy which is the Inner essence of TRT.

Barbara Ray, Ph.D.

This book is for everyone, for it is both valuable and beneficial to people in their personal growth and transformation, even if they have not yet studied The Radiance Technique®. To learn this technique, you will need to be taught by a fully qualified, currently certified Authorized Instructor. TRT cannot be learned from this or any book. (Please see the Addresses page for more information.)

The joy of participating in this Expanded Edition leads me to a re-awakening to the wonderful empowering this book and The Radiance Technique® bring to the world. First of all, I had the joy to be involved in the first-ever printing of the original manuscript in 1980. And in some of the years since then I have had the opportunity to assist as an editor in the preparation of the Expanded Edition. In the here now, I am in the midst of helping as an editor and proofreader with the new and even more expanded edition, and it has been a profoundly touching experience. As I read and reread these chapters, I am frequently filled with wonder at the profound wisdom that Dr. Barbara Ray has placed within these pages.

This book speaks to me anew each time I spend time with it. That, to me, is the true measure of a book–that it transcends the few years, in the sense of centuries and civilizations, during which it is printed and sold. This book offers power to any individual in the world, regardless of nationality or language, who feels powerless in the face of events and forces that seem greater than a human can bear. This book reminds me that The Radiance Technique empowers me to realize I *can* make a difference with every single energy, dark or light, that comes into my life. (1992)

Fred W. Wright Jr.
The Fourth Degree
Writer/Editor/Teacher

PART I

The most beautiful thing we can experience is the mysterious. It is the source of all true art and science.

Albert Einstein

1

Introduction: A New Beginning

Only that day dawns to which we are awake.

Thoreau

Think of it! Every day of your life represents an opportunity for a new beginning. Every breath you take is a rebirth, drawing in a new round of air connecting you to the universal vibrations of that particular moment. Exhaling is a letting go or a releasing of what has now become the past, and the new breath again keeps you in the "here now"–the eternal present.

Life is made of energy, and energy is in perpetual motion, moving in swirling spirals. Each moment in your life is a new part of the unfolding spiral of your own life's process. The very essence of life is motion–nothing is status quo. Movement and change are basic, natural laws of energy–of life.

The truth is that everything you do is for the first time. Of course, you do not forget what you have already learned. The natural flow is learning from the past, whether it was a year ago or a moment ago, and synthesizing this knowledge into your being. Each new breath spirals you on to a new experience. Every minute you are different from the one before. Some people are "awake" to this natural phenomenon. That is, some people are consciously aware of and in tune with this natural

rhythm of life-force energy running through them. Everything they do is done new, is personal, and is very much alive! These people can be called "masters."

You are a "master," too, deep within your Being–everyone is, although not everyone is "awake" to this aspect of themselves. Adaptability, flexibility, openness, acceptance, going with the natural flow, and the ability to perceive the Essence of all things are some "master" qualities which you could become Conscious of in an awakening process through ongoing use of The Radiance Technique®.

Now that you have this book about TRT, relax, make yourself comfortable, and allow yourself to be open to some new ideas. Make the reading of this book an opportunity for learning, growing, and transforming, as well as for integrating new concepts and affirming some you already had.

The first part of the book deals with the essence of The Radiance Technique®. Use your mind, your emotions, and your intuitions to grasp this perception–the insight of what TRT *in its essence* is–a precise energy science accessing transcendental, whole, harmless energy.

The second part of the book describes the uses of TRT in your daily life and the experiences many other people have had using this unique technique. All of the examples contain descriptions of uses of TRT but, ultimately, do not contain the experience itself. That experience you have to get directly through and within yourself.

You and I can talk endlessly about swimming, but the way we get the experience of swimming is by doing it. We can discuss many aspects of apples, but the way we really know the apple is by eating it. There is no single "experience" from using TRT. An experience one person has is not "right" and another person's "wrong." Their experiences are just different from each other. *All* the experiences with using TRT give insight to how it can and does work. TRT accesses a life-force, *Universal* energy. This Universal vibration is the "Dance of Life" energy.

As I mentioned in the preface, this book is divided into two parts and can be read in any order that suits you. For example, you might be especially interested in what use of TRT can do for you in helping to release excess stress or in relaxing you.

You might want to read the chapter "Stress, Relaxation and The Radiance Technique" first and then read the other chapters. Each chapter will give you insights to TRT helping you understand its unique process more fully. For that reason, I recommend that, ultimately, you read the whole book!

My basic approach was to go from the general context of TRT as a technique for energy-balancing, natural healing, maintaining positive wellness, higher consciousness, and ultimately Enlightenment to specific discussions of what TRT is and how it works, and examples of how it can be used in your daily life.

Part I gives a context for TRT in modern times as we move through a transitional phase into new stages of evolving consciousness. Then some basic guidelines are given for understanding the wholistic model and TRT, followed by discussions of what TRT is, how the technique works, and its possible origins.

Part II tells how TRT can be used in your daily life according to *your own personal needs*, shows how the basic principle underlying this technique can be applied to any disease or imbalance, and demonstrates that TRT does not interfere or conflict with medical treatment in any way. I have included a wide variety of individual cases demonstrating the benefits of TRT to facilitate your understanding.

Appendix A is a section of questions I have been asked about TRT, and answers.

Appendix B sketches some of the events in my life that led me to discover TRT and provided me with the expertise to identify what kind of energy science TRT is. In addition, teaching Seminars and extended work in healing/wholing and personal transformation gave me the fullness of direct experiences with TRT since 1978.

The verb "to heal" derives from an old English root meaning "to make whole." Throughout this book, I have used the word "wholing" as synonymous with healing to convey the idea of wholeness. I have also coined the term "Light-energy" in referring to the universal, life-force energy accessed by TRT. The activating-energy attunements of TRT tap you directly into this high-level natural Light-energy of a Cosmic order. You can then use this connection in the ways that are best suited to you

as a natural energy source for healing, wholing, and maintaining positive wellness and even for achieving in a natural way higher consciousness or what some call "Cosmic Consciousness." In modern physics, the question of consciousness has arisen in connection with quantum theory. As Robert Toben stated in *Space-Time and Beyond*, "Consciousness is the missing hidden variable in the structure of matter."

In discussing TRT both in this book and in public lectures and seminars, I try to convey what the essence of TRT is and how it works with as little interpretation *as is possible* because of the obvious limitations of words in discussing transcendental energy. TRT is a technique for connecting oneself to life-force, Universal energy and for applying this energy. What you do with TRT depends on your own individual needs as *your* life's process unfolds.

One of the meanings of the verb "to interpret" is "to translate." Everyone knows that in verbal interpretations, something is lost in the translation. When you describe an experience to a friend, even when you retell it in your own words, it is never quite the same as the original experience.

Interpretations tend to impose limits, putting things into square boxes rather than keeping them in the flow of naturally spiraling energy. Interpretations often include projections of your own psychological blocks and thereby alter or color what was really there. Interpretations also tend to create illusions, that is, they tend to keep you from seeing that *"what is, is."*

Interpretations often keep you locked into the past with closed doors and lead you to rigid categorizing. The closest I have been able to categorize TRT is to call it a self-help technique for healing, wholing, growth, and transformation, for expanding and awakening Consciousness, and for Enlightenment.

Some people have interpreted and categorized TRT as simply a body therapy. That is partly true. But as will be demonstrated throughout this book, TRT is more than just a body therapy. Others have interpreted and categorized TRT as occult. "Occult" is defined as "of, pertaining to, dealing with, or knowledgeable in supernatural influences, agencies or phenomena; beyond the realm of human comprehension; mysterious; inscrutable."[1] Only to the extent that Life itself is

mysterious is TRT occult. Even Albert Einstein acknowledged the mystery of life in his words, "The most beautiful thing we can experience is the mysterious. It is the source of all true art and science."[2]

Through the years, I have heard many other interpretations and partial truths expressed about TRT. Most of these interpretations simply reflect the limited knowledge and perspective of the persons making them.

As you continue to read, keep yourself open and absorb the material rather than interpreting it. Let the words guide you rather than block you, and let the meaning resonate and connect within you. In this way, you will discover for yourself some insights to what TRT is! If you take a TRT Seminar, you will have the direct, "no-words-in-between" experience of using TRT. TRT accesses in its essence a freeing, liberating, healing, natural Universal energy.

As outlined above, I have included in Appendix B some details of my journey in discovering TRT and how my academic studies enabled me to recognize it for what it is. Deep within me, I had known that this Ancient technique for activating from within a person a high order of Universal life energy was still on this planet. I just did not know where to find it. Gradually, certain events unfolded in my life that brought me in direct contact with The Radiance Technique, transforming my life and opening all the dimensions of Being that I had "known" were within us all.

2

Dawning of a "New Age" of Consciousness and The Radiance Technique®

There are "events" in the human mass, just as there are in the world of organic matter, or in the crust of the earth, or in the stellar universe; and so there are also certain privileged beings who are present at and share in such events.
Pierre Teilhard de Chardin

You and I are these privileged beings living together and sharing in one of the most profound moments of human evolution and history. We are living and participating in one of those "events" in the human mass to which Chardin was referring and to which has often been applied the term the "dawning of the Age of Aquarius." We seem to be in a profound transitional period, moving from what was called the Age of Pisces to that of Aquarius or from the Industrial Age to that of Technology or Space.

We are living in a time when civil unrest and political upheavals occur almost daily, when terrorists play power games with governments and with the lives of hostages, when

8

inflation soars seemingly out of control, when the assassin's gun aims indiscriminately at political and religious leaders, when many twentieth-century "Cassandras" cry doom for all of us, and when parents wonder what to do about a child's relationship with computerized machines. Yet in the midst of the worldwide confusion, conflict, and chaos and the harangue of the modern chorus of prophets chanting doom, a new civilization appears to be arising. A new pattern is emerging and is visible upon the horizon, marking the birthing and possible ascendance of a "new age" of expanded human Consciousness. What makes this particular phase we are experiencing so confusing yet so provocative, so frightening yet so inspiring, is the realization that profound change and transformation are stirring many of us individually and some in groups to the awakening of a new level of human consciousness possible all over this planet. Interestingly enough, the traditional symbolism for the Age of Aquarius is the water-bearer—a fully awakened person pouring water, representing knowledge, to everyone on this earth plane. Whoever drinks of the water will be transformed to a higher state of consciousness, a higher state of Being. This symbolism shows clearly that the Age of Aquarius is an age when all of humanity will have the opportunity to make a choice to grow, to change, and to transform.

The knowledge and the power to transform are available to everyone by learning to open from within to a higher order of energy and by *consciously* tapping or connecting to that inner power. On another level, the knowledge and power to transform are available to many nations in the famous formula $E = MC^2$ of Albert Einstein. The choice is ours whether to use our technology, power, and energy to create wars or peace, to foster hatred or unconditional love, or to annihilate ourselves or create a new world order. The key is in our consciousness. "To be or not to be?" is still the main issue for reflection by all of us.

It is helpful to know that this Aquarian Age will take approximately the next twenty-five hundred years to unfold; it will take many generations. When viewed from the wholistic perspective of hundreds of years, stages of this unfolding process into mankind's "new age" of a higher evolution of Consciousness are easier to identify and to relate to. The phase we are

currently in is that of the birthing or what some have called the transitional phase or passage to another cycle of human life and consciousness. The transition to this "new age" began during this past century, and new *light* is dawning everywhere on this planet. As Alvin Toffler so aptly and succinctly puts it in his book *The Third Wave*, "A new civilization is emerging in our lives, and blind men everywhere are trying to suppress it."[1] Then he emphatically reminds us that "the dawn of this new civilization is the single most explosive fact of our life-times."[2]

Periods of transition in human history as well as in individual lives are always characterized by conflict and confusions. The old patterns of being and the old ways of existing always resist the new patterns of becoming and the new ways of perceiving. So, too, in the current process of transformation, which is affecting our entire planet, the struggles, conflicts, despairs, and deaths indicate also signs of the birthing of a possible new phase of human evolution.

The single most outstanding feature of this "new age" of humanity is the awakening consciousness of mankind as a whole.

In *The Aquarian Conspiracy*, Marilyn Ferguson describes it as a "new mind—the ascendance of a startling world view that gathers into its framework breakthrough science and insights from earliest recorded thought." The Radiance Technique was rediscovered from man's past, an ancient science of Universal energy thousands of years old. TRT accesses within its process transcendental Light-energy. TRT is a precise, self-help, transformative technique which is both an art and a science that can be easily and safely learned by nearly anyone. In Chapter 8, the rediscovery of TRT as a tool for the evolving of Consciousness is traced.

Expanding Consciousness means going beyond the old limits and extending to a larger sphere. By analogy, to comprehend that the world encompasses more than the home, a child might be given a model of home, street, city, and state. As the child begins to understand a perspective bigger than his home, he can then be given an expanded model of state, plus many states, plus United States (country), plus other countries, and including the concept of "world" or "planet." To hold onto only

10

the model of "home" would be to limit severely our human capacity for conceptual growth. To include the understanding gained from the model of "home" but also to expand to the consciousness of "world" and ultimately to "universe" or "cosmos" would be to experience our innate capacity for continuous, unlimited expansion of Consciousness.

For nearly two hundred years, Isaac Newton's model of mechanical clockwork universe dominated modern physics. Newtonian law was essentially one of cause and effect, as demonstrated by billiard balls hitting one another and moving in a predictable pattern of response. The Newtonian perspective tended to be linear and mechanistic. But as scientific investigation continued, based for the most part on Newton's model, an increasing amount of data did not fit into that framework.

Early in this century, Einstein's special theory of relativity presented a new, expanded paradigm for comprehending the universe. The old model was not entirely wrong, but the new one offered by Einstein went beyond the limits set by Newton and forced a more inclusive, wholistic view. The new model that emerged has enabled scientists to gain an enormously increased comprehension of the universe. The transformations in our lives triggered by new physics reminds me of Dorothy's remark in the *Wizard of Oz*, "Goodness, Toto, I've a feeling we're not in Kansas anymore!" Likewise, these new perspectives have transformed our daily lives in a myriad of ways through technological advances applied from our kitchens to our offices and from our bodies to our spirits! I have a feeling we are not in the past anymore! A new paradigm by its larger perspective transforms old knowledge and unveils new dimensions for our exploration and experience. Manifesting in the dynamics of this new possibility of expanding Consciousness is the paradigmatic change from a mechanistic to a wholistic perspective. It is true, of course, that throughout human history certain individuals and even small, specialized groups have exhibited a "wholistic consciousness." A positive trend of today's world is that everywhere on this planet millions of people from all social, economic, professional, and educational levels are awake or are in the process of awakening to this model–this vision of wholeness.

11

Indeed, the evolutionary process of this new stage of humanity has already begun, and the ancient, Universal wisdom embodied within TRT has re-emerged as a transformative tool for energy balancing, for natural healing, for wholing, and for creating peace, joy, and love, and, ultimately, for achieving higher Consciousness and Enlightenment.

3

The Wholistic Model

The shift from the mechanistic to the holistic conception of reality is likely to result in a transformation of unprecedented dimension.

Fritjof Capra

The word "holistic," sometimes spelled with a "*w*" as "wholistic," derives from the Greek word *holos* meaning to view something from the functional interrelationship of all its parts. In essence, the wholistic paradigm offers a dynamic model of seeing and considering everything as an organic whole. The dictionary definition of "whole" includes the concepts of "containing all component parts, not disjoined but unified and restored, healthy and *healed*." In skillfully applying principles of wholeness in your daily life, you will begin to develop a perspective that increases your inner sensitivity to your entire being–physically, emotionally, mentally, and spiritually. Likewise, through the process of shifting your model to one of wholeness, you will be able to see yourself with clarity in your external relationships with other people and with your environment. In shifting to a wholistic model, you will be expanding to a consciousness that will affect profoundly your entire living process. You will be opening yourself to vast insights

13

and to a new sense of confidence in the unfolding of your life process.

The wholistic perspective shifts your vision to be inclusive rather than exclusive; it expands rather than restricts; it is spherical rather than square; and it allows you to see the whole pattern, putting the pieces into perspective relative to each other rather than as isolated, unconnected parts.

On paper, the wholistic model is a circle or a mandala that appears static, flat, and two-dimensional. In reality and in consciousness, this model is in motion like the counterclockwise, spiraling energy of a spiral galaxy. Life is motion. Life is multidimensional.

With the wholistic model, you are able to see and to intuit the interconnectedness of all things. You can see the natural flow of energy. From ancient to modern times, Eastern mystics have spoken of the essential unity and interrelatedness of all natural phenomena. All things were seen as a manifestation of basic oneness and as a part of a greater, cosmic whole. Twentieth-century physics now reveals that this wholeness appears to be a universal reality. In *The Tao of Physics* Fritjof Capra states that the study of subatomic particles has revealed "the same insight—that the constituents of matter and the basic phenomena involving them are all interconnected, interrelated and interdependent; that they cannot be understood as isolated entities, but only as integrated parts of the whole."

In the personal search for Self, the journey often begins with outer forms and tends to move to inner levels of experience and knowledge. So we will begin with the concepts of wholistic health and keep in mind that these principles apply to the physical dimension of our being as well as to the emotional, mental, and spiritual aspects of ourselves.

The concept of wholistic health and living can best be expressed in the statements: "The whole is greater than the sum of its parts" and "A house is more than a collection of bricks." The wholistic approach to your life means looking at all of the parts together as well as that which sustains the harmony among the parts. "That which sustains the harmony" is the dimension I will refer to throughout this book as "spiritual." The implication, wholistically speaking, is that in addition to our physical, emotional, or mental experiences, life

consists of an essence called the "spiritual dimension," and everyone has it!

In using wholistic principles in reference to your health, you will be shifting your paradigm, that is, your model, from a mechanistic (monistic) one to a wholistic one. The mechanistic view of health that has literally dominated modern Western medicine viewed the body as a machine with parts that are to be treated separately. The emphasis is on the physical body with little or no attention to the emotional, mental, and spiritual dimensions of ourselves. The mechanistic approach is not wrong in that it recognizes a need to treat an injured or diseased physical part; but it tends to exclude the greater truth that *all* parts of your being must be activated in the healing process or in the process of maintaining positive wellness and wholeness. In contrast, the wholistic approach takes into account as many aspects of the individual as possible. For purposes of illustration, let us assume that as a child you fell while playing at school. The physical injury you received was as minor as a bruise or a scratch. You were treated for the physical injury and sent back to class. Now imagine that while falling you were feeling not only the physical pain but you were also having the emotional response of embarrassment, inferiority, and shame when your classmates laughed at your fall. Add to this your mental response of wishing you were not there or perhaps thinking you had done something wrong and were being punished by God. Now imagine that many years have passed and as an adult you are faced with a difficult injury or disease. Your mind has long forgotten the little episode at school, but your present physical plight elicits the old feelings of embarrassment, inferiority, and shame. You spend a great deal of time wishing you did not have the condition, and you feel punished by God or possibly even deny such a force as Divine Intelligence in the cosmos!

In approaching this situation from a wholistic perspective, all of the above-mentioned responses would be taken into consideration. Not only would the physical injury or disease be treated with a variety of physical therapies, but, in addition, therapies for the emotional, mental, and spiritual bodies would be explored. To quote that well-known phrase, "A house

15

is more than a collection of bricks." You, indeed, are more than a collection of bones, veins, and organs!

The mechanistic approach tends to treat symptoms, whereas the wholistic approach looks for recurrent patterns. Symptoms and causes are examined and treated, and the individual involved has an opportunity for growth on many levels of being. Manifestations of disease, pain, and other signals of distress are regarded as important information about conflicts, imbalances in energy use, and disharmony of elements within the person. Disease on any level of your being is viewed as a process for expanding your consciousness by increasing your sensitivity to the interrelated energy fields of the body-emotion-mind-spirit dynamic. In the wholistic model, the primary concern is with the integrated, whole person. To settle for less in your life is to limit your innate potential for growth and to deny *your* birthright to health, wholeness, and Enlightenment.

In the mechanistic model of healing, emphasis is placed primarily on the ability of someone else to heal you. You were perhaps taught from early childhood, whenever you were ill, broken down, or in some way not physically whole, to give someone else the responsibility for making you well or for "fixing" you. The primary message you received was to go to the outside for healing and surrender to someone else *your power* for restoring your own health. In that process, you could easily experience a sense of loss of your own "life power," resulting in feelings of helplessness, depression, and defeat. You could grow to resent the physician who is attempting to help you if healing results are not forthcoming as expected or additional complications arise. In such a state, you can begin to feel that you are worthless and powerless and have no control whatever over your own life process.

Again, the mechanistic approach is not wrong in its assumption that other people possibly can help you. Its perspective, however, is not large enough. In contrast, the wholistic model has as one of its basic tenets the concept that *you* assume responsibility for your healing process and maintenance of health. The assumption is that, as a living, active individual, you *do* have certain significant and fundamental controls over

your life, that you *can* make intelligent choices for yourself, and that you *do* have the power, within you, to restore and maintain your health. The wholistic model shifts the responsibility of wellness to the individual and thereby presents the opportunity for you to realize that in the most essential ways *you are in charge of your life!* In shifting your personal consciousness to a wholistic model, you would not necessarily eliminate seeking assistance and guidance from others. But the relationships between you and the other persons would be one of interaction, support, and interrelating rather than one of dependency, powerlessness, and hopelessness.

In addition, it is important to note that in the traditional mechanistic approach, treatment generally begins when a disease has manifested tangibly but that little or no attention is given to preventive techniques or to the development of a science of wholeness. In going to a larger perspective, the wholistic approach deals not only with the manifested disease but also emphasizes preventive techniques and encourages you as an individual to develop an approach to positive wellness and wholeness that is best suited to your particular needs, preferences and lifestyle. A leading exponent of wholistic medicine, Dr. Harold Bloomfield, maintains, "It may be convincingly argued that modern medicine has achieved unprecedented success in treating disease but has proven virtually incapable of promoting health."[1]

In shifting from the mechanistic to the wholistic model, you will need to select tools that are inherently designed to expand consciousness on all levels of your being–techniques that activate and promote integration of the body-emotion-mind-spirit dynamic. As Marilyn Ferguson appropriately states, "The difference between transformation by accident and transformation by a system is like the difference between lightning and a lamp. Both give illumination, but one is dangerous and unreliable, while the other is relatively safe, directed, available."[2] The Radiance Technique, in and of itself, is a complete, safe system for personal healing, wholing, and transforming which simultaneously includes your body-emotion-mind-spirit dynamic. In its essence, TRT accesses a natural, whole, Universal energy and provides a way of activating and amplifying this

Radiant, Cosmic power within you. As a natural, energy-balancing method, TRT is safe and easy to use.

TRT is also a special technique for directing natural energy in such a way that your entire being is transformed and illuminated *according to the process which is uniquely and naturally yours*. Unlike many other techniques and therapies, TRT can be used effectively in combination with other methods for healing and transformation. In expanding to a wholistic approach to your health and life, TRT provides a direct method for activating your inner power. With use of TRT, you can naturally accept responsibility for your own health and well-being. Using TRT also helps minimize your sense of helplessness and powerlessness when faced with physical, emotional, mental, or spiritual struggles and imbalances. In addition, when used as instructed, TRT provides you with an essential preventive technique and a means of developing positive wellness and wholeness maintenance regardless of your age.

In summary, it can be seen in answering the question, "What is wholistic health and living?" the wholistic model offers an approach to living that emphasizes the importance of integrating into every aspect of your life process all levels of your being—physical, emotional, mental, and spiritual. In applying this wholistic model to health, healing, and everyday living, all dimensions of your self are taken into account as important even though different in nature. The wholistic perspective gives you an awareness of yourself as "uniquely *you*" as well as a sensitivity to a larger vision of yourself in relation to others as you journey through your life's unfolding process.

Your expanding consciousness will also allow you to become sensitive in a new way to your oneness with all people. You will gain a deeper appreciation of the wonderful diversity in manifested life forms. By living your life from a perspective of wholeness you will each day be able to celebrate the realization of a new awareness of our basic unity within our diversity.

The self-help aspect of TRT is a unique way of getting in touch with the life-force energy and of promoting your own healing and wholing, of maintaining positive wellness, and of naturally opening yourself to a higher consciousness. TRT can easily, safely, and effectively be combined with whatever other therapies you are using on a daily basis.

4

Universal Energy in
The Radiance Technique®

The Radiance Technique® accesses universal energy and puts your consciousness in touch with qualities of wholeness such as clarity, radiant power, universal love, joy, abundance, and Light.
Barbara Ray

Modern scientists have analyzed the world with an amazing degree of sophistication. The material world has been divided into finer and finer particles only to discover that deep inside the tunnel, at the ultimate center of "what is," we find energy/vibration. We have discovered the simple truth that energy/vibration precedes matter just as emotions and thoughts precede action. More than forty-five hundred years ago, the Chinese postulated that a subtle system of life-sustaining energy circulates through living physical bodies. This energy/vibration is called "ki" and is pronounced "key." *Ki* is the basic life-force energy or *vital energy* found in all living things and has just that meaning as the suffix on the word, reiki. "Rei" denotes cosmic, universal energy and "ki" refers to the life energy of the physical, outer levels of the self. The term conveys the concept

of the energy of the Whole, the aligning of the part (ki) with the Whole, Universal (rei) in an ever-expanding principle of dynamic interaction.

Basic to all Oriental healing arts is the concept that *ki* is the vital life force upon which physical life is dependent. In Chinese *ki* is *Chi*, in Hindu it is *prana*, and in English breath and ectoplasm come closest to the essential meaning of *ki*. Russian researchers call it *bioplasmic* energy, Hippocrates called it *nature's life force*, the Kahunas called it *mana*, and Christ called it *light*. It has also been called *cosmic energy, bioenergy,* and *vital force*. The harmony, amount, and balance of this vital energy of *ki* within you is essential for the health and the proper functioning of your being in this life. *Ki* energy is finer than electricity but is related to it. The state of *ki* in your system relates to the body-mind harmony or disharmony you are experiencing in your daily life. Indeed, the balance, amount, and quality of your *ki* is influenced by a variety of aspects such as air quality, food, amounts and kinds of stress, heredity factors, and environmental conditions. To maintain a balance in your health physically, emotionally, mentally, and spiritually, you need an unpolluted source of whole energy to restore your vital energy.

At your birth, you have a certain level of *ki*, vital energy. As you live each day, you tend to expend varying amounts of energy. Therefore, each day you need natural sources for replenishing your energy expenditures. When you continue to expend more energy than you restore on all levels of your being, you often are faced with physical, emotional, and mental imbalances or diseases. With low or drained vital energy, you are inclined toward physical fatigue and illness as well as emotional and mental exhaustion. You can become irritable, angry, hostile, and even paranoid. You can have difficulty thinking clearly, and you can be constantly tired, exhausted, and even depressed. Indeed, in such depleted states, it is difficult for you to feel spiritually uplifted and inspired.

Simply a generic term, rei-ki can be used by anyone to describe anything. The Radiance Technique® (TRT) is a registered term for clearly denoting this particular method for using universal life energy and differentiates it from "other

reiki things." The Radiance Technique® is a specific technique for restoring and balancing your natural life-force energy. TRT is neither a dogma nor a religion but is a complete, scientific method for self-healing and for maintaining your health and sense of well-being physically, emotionally, mentally, and spiritually. TRT is an effective technique for prevention of diseases and energy imbalances on all levels of your being. TRT is also a unique, highly effective tool for personal transformation, growth, and change. TRT is a natural energy-balancing and renewing method that can be used in conjunction with any other technique of health-care treatment as well as with any other personal growth therapy. TRT does not conflict with traditional medicine but can be used with it or as an additional source for restoring vital energy and promoting health and well-being.

TRT method of natural healing is designed to strengthen systematically your absorption of vital life energy. When tensions develop in your physical body or blocks occur in your mind or emotions, your flow of vital energy can stagnate and be depleted excessively. You begin, then, to break down physically and emotionally. You see things as if in a fog and sometimes feel as though you will never recover. The constant stress and daily pressures typical of modern life often result in our being increasingly alienated from natural healing energies. By using TRT in your daily life, you will gradually be able to regain your energy balance. Once you have accumulated enough *ki* for your normal maintenance and functioning, you will be able to reserve and conserve energy. The Radiance Technique puts energy into your body in a specific manner. Use of TRT regulates and balances the *ki* flow as needed specifically by *your* body. By balancing and restoring your vital energy, *ki*, you will be working directly with natural energy.

TRT puts you in direct contact with natural, whole energy and in touch with the flow of *ki* in your being. In using TRT, you will be working to heal the inner causes of diseases, imbalances, and disorders rather than merely treating symptoms. Symptoms are important signals that something is off balance and that you are losing energy without sufficient renewal. For healing to occur, however, the cause of the symptom must be

21

treated or released. Therefore, in using TRT you may also need to work with the outer and inner conditions that tend to influence your *ki* state on a daily basis.

The Radiance Technique helps you to regain balance physically, emotionally, mentally, and spiritually. The use of TRT will involve you directly with your own healing and daily renewing process. If you are not actually experiencing an illness, you will be restoring and balancing energy that you have depleted in the course of your normal, daily activities. For positive, ongoing wellness, TRT is one of the most efficient relaxation and stress-reduction techniques available to modern man. TRT has the additional benefits of requiring no special conditions or equipment except *yourself* and a seminar of instruction by an authorized instructor. Once you have learned this unique technique, it can be used throughout the day in a variety of locations and situations. Using The Radiance Technique, indeed, is as natural as breathing.

PART II

Health is a precious thing . . . the only thing indeed that deserves to be pursued at the expense not only of time, sweat, labor, worldly goods but of life itself; since without health life becomes a burden and an affliction.

Montaigne

9

The Radiance Technique®
In Your Daily Life

Any imbalance is experienced as a need
to correct this imbalance.
Frederick S. Perls

TRT is for activating and accessing universal life energy of a higher order within you, and it is a specific method for applying this energy and balancing yourself and healing yourself. One of the basic tenets of wholistic health and living is accepting responsibility for your own health, sense of well-being, and evolving consciousness. TRT is a unique method for unlocking the powers that can be found within all of us and can be easily used in your daily life in numerous ways. TRT gives you a direct means of restoring vital energy as you deplete energy during your daily activities, whatever they may be. Depleting or exhausting your vital energy throughout the day *without* adequately and fully replenishing it results in imbalances that affect your physical, emotional, mental, spiritual dynamic.

TRT is *not* a substitute for your need to restore energy with natural foods, nor is it a substitute for exercise appropriate to your particular lifestyle. TRT provides an access to an essential source of natural energy that enhances all of your activities. For

57

example, many runners and other athletes have used TRT for restoring energy burned up in sports and other vigorous exercise activities.

TRT can be used on the spot to energize yourself no matter where you are or what you are doing. This unique technique can be used effectively in balancing your energy physically, emotionally, and mentally as you progress through daily situations and interactions. TRT is also effective in eliminating or controlling the effects of bruises, bumps, burns, and bleeding from cuts or other accidents that might happen to you in the course of daily activities.

Headaches are one of the most common complaints in our contemporary society. Studies show that Americans consume millions of aspirins and other pain-relief pills each day. The feedback I get most frequently about TRT use is its effectiveness in releasing headaches and other pain. Migraines respond positively when TRT is used consistently over a period of several weeks or months, and the migraine pattern can usually be eliminated completely when the technique is used as instructed. Headaches are important signals of accumulated negative stress or imbalanced energy. TRT promotes negative stress release and energy balancing as well as positive stress responses so that you are healing the cause and eliminating the effect.

Once you have learned TRT, you will be able to apply its basic principles to any disease or energy imbalance you are experiencing in the daily course of your life. With TRT, it is possible to obtain relief from allergies, arthritis, and other chronic imbalances. By using TRT *as instructed*, it is possible to build a high level of reserve energy so that during more distressful times in your life you will have something to "fall back on" without completely draining yourself. With TRT, your natural resiliency is enhanced. Continual depletion of vital energy without replenishing it adequately tends to run down your immune system. The immune system is the body's natural defense against disease, and TRT is a harmless and supportive method for balancing and enhancing the immune system.

Part II of this book gives some specific uses of TRT in promoting energy balancing, healing, wholing and positive wellness. Since researchers now are able to relate high levels of negative stress to deficient immune systems tending to result in disease and imbalances, special attention is given to stress, relaxation, and using TRT. Releasing and reducing negative stress while promoting positive stress responses appears to be an essential *key* to balanced energy, positive wellness, wholeness, and even Enlightenment. Keep in mind as you are reading that *all of the principles* of using TRT *apply* to *all* diseases and imbalances *whether or not* I make a specific reference to one that is of special interest to you. TRT accesses Universal, Radiant Energy which can be applied safely to any living organism. These chapters also provide other examples of benefits received by individuals through use of TRT, whether used alone or in combination with medical treatments and/or other therapies.

The chapter on death, dying, and TRT is intended to help you understand the dying and death process as a natural and highly significant part of each of our lives. One of the first and perhaps the most difficult lessons in healing and wholing is that of letting go of rigid attachments to expectations and end results. Life is a *process, not a result.* Healing, wholing, and balancing energy is a process, and dying is a natural part of the life experience. Dying and renewing or rebirthing into other states of being are natural cycles within which our whole life experience exists. TRT is an ancient wisdom that can be used now to support and to help guide ourselves and others through the dying process.

TRT goes along *naturally* with whatever your own individual process is in the "here-now." The key to immortality is in awakening Consciousness, not in holding onto outer forms, limited patterns, or closed systems, whether they be physical, emotional, or mental. A step in awakening your consciousness is *trusting* in your life's unfolding process, expressed in contemporary jargon, "going with the flow." The Radiance Technique helps you *where you are* and gently beckons you to opening each day of your life.

Here is a wonderful Sufi tale for reflection:

> *The great Sufi sage, Mullah Nasrudin, once entered a shop and demanded of the keeper, Have you ever seen me before?" "No!" responded the shopkeeper promptly. "Then," cried Nasrudin, "how do you know it is me?"*

59

10

Stress, Relaxation and
The Radiance Technique®

*There are two roads to survival: fight
and adaptation. And most often adaptation is the more successful.*
Hans Selye

Stress as defined by medical researchers describes the daily
wear and tear on our bodies, emotions, minds, and spirits. Dr.
Hans Selye, director of the Institute on Experimental Medicine
and Surgery at the University of Montreal and the leading
authority on stress, defines stress "as the body's nonspecific
response to any demand made upon it."[1] In and of itself, the
stress response is neither good nor bad, and Dr. Selye's definition clearly shows that the stress response cannot be eliminated. Stress, however, can be divided into two basic catego-
ries: positive stress responses, which bring us joy, balance,
wellness, and wholeness, and negative stress responses, which
Dr. Selye calls *distress*, which drain your energy, sap your
vitality, lower your resistance, and make you vulnerable to
disease on all levels of your being. Current research indicates
that when distress is prolonged or excessive in your life, you
begin suffering from physical, emotional, and mental

disharmonies. You age prematurely, and you could experience chronic, debilitating, physical conditions. Emotionally, you lose your ability to cope. You suffer anxiety, depression, fatigue, and irritability. Mentally, you become confused and unable to think clearly and to make choices and decisions rationally. Spiritually, you feel empty inside, bored, cynical, and, essentially, unfulfilled. Stress can accumulate to such an extent that a person can no longer cope and illnesses develop. Research on the relationship between stress and disease over many years has shown that a connection does exist.

Dr. Herbert Benson, in his book *The Relaxation Response*, points out that the human nervous system is designed to handle certain amounts of stress. The nervous system is set to react to external threats in what has been termed the "fight or flight" response. Modern man, however, often finds himself in many situations in which he inhibits his natural fight or flight response. When your boss ridicules your work, or a spouse or parent constantly attacks you verbally, or any other number of external demands are put on you daily, your body has a distress response. Unfortunately, in many of these situations, fight or flight is not appropriate. Consequently, you constantly suppress your responses to stress. What results is chronic distress, stress that is held in and not released. As Dr. Carl Simonton, leading authority in cancer research, puts it, "And chronic stress, it is increasingly recognized, plays a significant role in many illnesses."[2]

Dr. Harold Bloomfield, a leading exponent of the wholistic approach, lists the major symptoms of excessive stress as including difficulty falling asleep or sleeping through the night, tension headaches, free-floating anxiety, feeling all wound up, feeling down in the dumps, chronic fatigue, pouches or dark circles under eyes, worry, inability to concentrate, irritability, frequent indigestion, frequent constipation, frequent colds, frequent angry outbursts, and excessive drinking, smoking, and eating. Certain bodily changes accompany unreleased distress and have a detrimental, sometimes devastating, effect on our health and sense of well-being. These changes include internal chemical reactions, hormonal changes, muscular tensions, increased heart rate, accelerated breathing, circulation difficulties, tension to our internal glands and organs, anxiety, and depression. There is much evidence to demonstrate the physical effects of stress. And, in addition, Dr. Selye's research has shown a definite connection between emotional and mental chronic stress and suppression or deterioration of the immune system. Without doubt, there is a significant link between our physical, emotional, mental and spiritual bodies. Physical distress tends to trigger emotional and mental distress and vice versa.

In our modern societies, we have to learn how to deal with distress-causing elements in our daily lives. First, we need to learn how to identify *what is causing* our negative stress accumulation. Our physical environment itself can be a high-level source of negative stress. External factors such as polluted air, food, and water, overcrowded conditions, and high noise levels increase our distress. Take, for example, the issue of noise and stress. Most of us experience the constant noise from motorized vehicles and machines. There are the sounds of people everywhere, of doors slamming, cars screeching, and planes flying overhead. In our homes and those of our neighbors, there are fairly constant noises from televisions, stereos, radios, and an unbelievable assortment of rumbling appliances, some of which never turn off, as well as the persistent ringing of telephones. Likewise, we must take into consideration that our emotional responses to high-level, constant noise can also be distressful. Typical responses are anger, irritation, aggressiveness, frustration, and anxiety.

Studies have shown that high-density and/or prolonged noises can be devastating to our wholeness. Dr. Dale Hattis of the Massachusetts Institute of Technology concluded that "loud noises may increase the adhesiveness of platelets in the blood to each other and that may contribute to long-term chronic arteriosclerosis–hardening of the arteries."[3]

Noise level and constancy as a source of distress in our daily lives is obviously just one area of our environment we would need to consider in assessing stress factors affecting each one of us.

In following a wholistic approach to health and living, you would examine all possible distress factors in your life. You should include not only your physical environment but also your personal relationships, your basic attitudes about life and your fellowman, your job or career activities, and your personal interests. I recommend that you begin now. Make a list of the negative stress-related symptoms you tend to exhibit most frequently. Then, begin a list of possible *causes* for these symptoms. Include physical as well as emotional, mental, and spiritual causes. In this process, you are beginning your personal journey in searching for Self. Working with finding the causes of blocks or distress that could be keeping you from your own unique, self-actualizing process begins another level of personal growth and expression for you. Discovering who you really are, getting in touch with your true self, expanding your sphere of consciousness, and *consciously* becoming one with your source is an incredibly sacred, beautiful journey toward wholeness.

In this process, you will need appropriate techniques designed inherently to promote positive stress responses and to help you release the effects of accumulated negative stress when the basic fight or flight response is not socially acceptable. In reference to dealing with stress, Dr. Simonton stated, "The key is the need to adapt to *change*, whether or not that change is in a positive or negative direction."[4] Physically, you will be moving toward a level of fitness suitable to your needs. You will be learning to renew and sustain a balance of natural energy. Emotionally, you will be moving toward a sense of well-being, an intrinsic happiness, and experiences of confidence, spontaneity, and optimism. You will be moving away from constant depression, anger, worry, and anxiety. Mentally, you will be expanding to clarity in thinking, and you will be healing old fears, inhibitions, and hang-ups, and you will be learning to deal with stress in new ways. Spiritually, you will be opening the doors to a wider sphere of Consciousness. You will be expanding to touching directly into your source of unconditional love, of unlimited strength, and of compassion. You will be becoming the authentic, genuine, real you!

The Radiance Technique is, in and of itself, complete and one that promotes distress releasing and full relaxation, both externally and internally. In using TRT, you are *naturally*, without force or without any artificial means, promoting positive stress responses throughout your entire being. Simultaneously, by doing a TRT hands-on session each day, you are releasing accumulated negative stress.

One woman, Dorothy,* had been undergoing dramatic changes in her life. Within seven months, she had lost her husband in a job-related accident and her youngest son to leukemia. When she came to a TRT Seminar, she was visibly exhausted and had dark circles and big bags under her eyes. Her vitality level was extremely low, and her health had been deteriorating at a rapid rate. She began using TRT as instructed on a daily basis. She had been to several doctors and one chiropractor and had tried psychotherapy for several months. Nothing seemed to help. At this point, her enthusiasm for TRT left much to be desired, but a friend had suggested the technique to her. She was so low that she had nothing to lose. As instructed, she began using TRT on a daily basis–sometimes several times a day. Within two weeks, the change in her appearance and attitude was so profound that even her friends had difficulty recognizing her. She has been using TRT for nearly two years now and has been able to change her response, gradually to release distress accumulated throughout her life, to benefit more from her psychotherapy, and to create a new, stimulating, and fulfilling cycle in her life.

TRT accesses universal, life, Light-energy, and in the series of transmissions given in the seminar your ability to tap this source energy is natural, direct, and amplified. The *connection* is made every single time as long as you are touching into something that is *alive*–be it yourself, a loved one, a pet, or plants. Once you have received the authentic TRT attunements, absolutely *nothing* can interfere with your new ability to tap life, Light-energy as long as the receiver is alive and as long as you actually use the technique. Having learned TRT, you will be carrying with you *at all times* and in every situation and location a technique that can be used on the spot for stress

In most cases, pseudonyms (fictitious names) have been used to protect individual privacy. In every other aspect, the facts of the cases are unchanged.

releasing. In addition, The Radiance Technique promotes energy-balancing, energy-renewing, positive stress responses and gives the *key* to adapting to change in your life, whether that change is negative or positive.

When distress is accumulated in your system as a result of the rigors of modern life, personal relationships, and life's process itself, you can use TRT for a few minutes in your office, in your car, riding on a bus, in a grocery store, while standing in lines, or virtually anywhere. TRT requires no special equipment, no altered states of consciousness, no special preparations or clothes, and no special moods or locations. TRT is not a dogma, not a religion, and not dependent on whether or not you believe in it. When this energy connection is put into motion, it works automatically just as your breath works without your thoughts or belief. At your birth, you were moved from one environment to another, and a connection was made with life on this plane. In a similar way, TRT amplifies the connection with universal energy, focuses the energy flow through your hands (although other focus points have been used, such as feet), and provides a specific technique that promotes positive stress responses and consciousness expansion and supports your process toward wholeness. TRT accesses whole energy, and that energy, ultimately, is Light. TRT literally puts you in direct contact with Light energy and lets you apply this Light-energy from the inside to the outside physical body.

A legal secretary began using TRT to help some of the attorneys in her office with muscular tensions, headaches, and other distress symptoms such as frustration, fatigue, and irritability. After a couple of weeks, everyone in this office of four top Atlanta attorneys, three legal secretaries, and one receptionist noticed a profound difference in attitude; all had increased energy levels and increased ability to cope with daily stress factors. She reported that the atmosphere in the entire office changed. It was not as "heavy" as it had been and seemed "light." With TRT so much in demand, she began losing her coffee break time and lunch hour. Finally, she suggested that each of them take a TRT Seminar, so that each could use the technique directly without relying on her.

One young man, who commutes to work in New York by subway each day, wrote to thank me for the TRT Seminar. He reported that he began using this technique during his thirty-minute subway ride going to and from work. He stated further, "I was amazed at the relief I got from anxiety about my job, about going to that office and dealing with my co-workers. My general energy level increased. Each evening while riding home and using TRT, I seemed to regenerate myself and I would arrive home feeling relaxed. It definitely had a positive effect on my family life."

Consider the following letter, reprinted in full, written by a successful businesswoman in Atlanta:

> I want to thank you again for the two sessions of TRT I have had to date. I honestly did not believe the process would work; my first reaction was that TRT was only a sort of metaphysical placebo and therefore couldn't possibly be effective on me as I tend to be much more pragmatic. As you recall, when I came to you for my first session, I was suffering the conglomerate of ill symptoms that has been best termed "executive stress"—I was exhausted, my entire body ached, my mind was disorganized, I was emotionally drained, and I felt a little nauseous. I was too tired to sleep. I was having difficulty handling my business operations efficiently. After an hour of TRT hands-on, the nausea was gone, my mental clarity had returned, and I felt energetic, objective, relaxed, and filled with a new sense of purpose. I went home and was able to plan a new administrative strategy which has greatly enhanced my business operations. It was as though you had put me in touch with the best of myself. Thank you again for the sessions. TRT should be available through every medical, chiropractic, and mental health facility in this country. Your fees are small price to pay for such impressive results. I don't know how TRT works, but it works; that's all that counts in my book!

One evening I stopped by a hospital to give one of my clients a hands-on session of TRT before her surgery the next morning. A tumor had been discovered in her uterus, cancer was suspected, and she would be undergoing a complete hysterectomy.

When I entered her room, I noticed immediately her radiance and calmness. She told me she had been using TRT on herself all afternoon amid the blood tests and physical preparations. From inside, fear, anxiety, depression, and terror had begun to get a hold on her. Then she remembered what I had instructed in TRT Seminar—always use TRT in highly distressful situations, *no matter where you are.* Using TRT, she could feel herself stabilizing emotionally and mentally almost immediately. She became interested in the preparatory activities, she relaxed, she was participating, she was even able to laugh more objectively at some of the routine procedures, and she talked with one of the attending nurses about this unique technique, TRT.

After the surgery, the woman kept on using daily TRT. I visited her two more times, and she was thrilled with her positive recovery process. She was aware of the renewed, vital energy being restored in her system. She knew she was healing and wholing on all levels of her being. She commented that she had never been so relaxed in her life, and yet she was in a hospital undergoing major surgery. It was a *real* growth process for her!

One woman from Smyrna, Georgia, whose entire family, including her husband, a ten-year-old, and an eight-year-old son, took the TRT Seminar, wrote:

> When I use TRT, I get very sleepy and relaxed. Sometimes I will go to sleep in the middle of the hands-on session. I am not one to see things or to hear things that are not there, but during some of these sessions, I see WHITE Light in various forms. . . . [my husband] gets immediate relief for his headaches with TRT.

Another woman wrote the following letter:

> It seems that there was hardly a day I can remember that I wasn't stressed and anxious. I had a chronic bladder infection and off and on suffered from severe migraine headaches. I knew those conditions were not normal but even modern medicine and psychiatry didn't seem to help. I felt helpless and often hopeless.

The quality of my life and vitality was at a minimum and my life had but little meaning. I heard about TRT and hoped it would help my bladder. Well, it did more than that. I was a changed person. My anxiety level went down, my migraines decreased, and my appreciation for life increased a hundredfold. I laughed more, was less tense, and was much more patient with myself and others. I love The Radiance Technique hands-on sessions I give myself. . . . it is the highlight of my day.

One man in his mid-thirties who took TRT told the class that he worked a day job as well as an evening job in order to support his family and cope with inflation. He was, however, exhausted. A friend who had received enormous benefits from TRT had recommended the seminar to him. He was totally skeptical about it, but he was *sure* that he was tired of being tired! After the first Attunement of TRT First Degree and instructions, he left for his all-night job. The next afternoon he came to the class very excited. He said that he had nearly fallen asleep on the job, but, as soon as he used the technique as instructed, he could feel his energy being restored. In thirty hours, he had managed to get only four hours sleep but found he could again stabilize and re-energize himself in twenty minutes by using TRT. He told us that TRT reminded him of the statement in a TV commercial for batteries, which ended with "energize me."

A student in his mid-thirties at a local university reported that with use of TRT he could concentrate more completely on his assignments and was doing much better in test situations, which usually triggered in him anxiety, tenseness, and mental blocking. By doing fifteen minutes of TRT hands-on before tests, he found his anxiety diminished, his mind cleared, and his confidence enhanced. He is also involved in sports and found TRT helpful on the spot for strains, bruises, tensions, and centering himself.

A young woman had a nervous disposition, involving tension and anxiety, and developing nearly daily severe headaches. Her father-in-law had benefitted enormously from using TRT and recommended she take the seminar. Within only two weeks after she completed the course, everyone she knew was amazed at the positive transformation in her personality. She was relaxed, was coping entirely differently with her family and friends, and was free from the tension and pain caused by the formerly severe headaches. She said that TRT was practical, effective, simple to use, did not require extra money for additional accessories, and did not cause conflicts with her husband. She was sure that using TRT had resulted in her personal transformation because nothing else new had been introduced into her life. She said she had gained "peace inside."

One of the additional positive benefits of TRT is that it can be used *along with* medical therapies and other techniques for healing and wholing. I have taught this Energy Science to many medical doctors, to osteopaths, to chiropractors, to massage experts, to dentists, to nurses, and to many others involved in various aspects of health care. One man, who had been a transcendental meditator, found The Radiance Technique "most enlightening" when used with his mantra. An expert yoga instructor verified that she combined use of TRT with some of the yoga positions and found her experiences more vivid, even more profound—"truly spiritual and enlightening."

A Rolfer found that TRT added a "special powerful but gentle" touch to his rolfing technique. A medical doctor said that with TRT he is able to transmit healing energy directly to his patients now even while talking with them. Another medical doctor reported that, in just a few minutes using TRT, he could reduce a patient's stress responses of tension, anxiety, and pain. Many psychologists have found TRT to be indispensable in helping to calm a patient in any anxiety attack and in promoting trust in the special relationship between client and therapist. Many cancer patients have found this Universal Energy Science to be extremely effective in diminishing and, in some case, in eliminating the often devastating side effects of radiation, chemotherapy and other drugs. Many have used TRT to restore natural energy depleted by drugs, surgery, and long or chronic illnesses. The Radiance Technique in *no way* conflicts with medical procedures but rather offers an often badly needed source of vital energy to help promote the healing process and relieve feelings of helplessness.

Not only is TRT a beneficial technique that can be used in combination with other methods, but it also can be applied while you are watching television, talking on the phone, meeting with others, and even resting. I have gotten into the habit of using TRT now when I am watching the evening news programs, which often are filled with distressful commentaries on our modern society! One woman expressed it this way, "No matter where I am or what I am doing, I work in a little use of TRT on myself. At my company's weekly business meeting, which is always highly pressured, highly tense, and highly charged, I stay relaxed, stress-free, and clear-headed while everyone else gets angry, anxious, and tense. I used to leave those meetings with severe headaches but now I use TRT, respond and interact calmly, and leave the meeting feeling good!"

One of the most relaxing and negative-stress-releasing combinations I have found and strongly recommend for promoting stress responses, healing, and wholeness is that of doing TRT while listening to certain music. For example, Steven Halpern, a nationally-known composer, creates what he has termed "anti-frantic" music. His scientific approach to music results in the creation of sounds that are designed to resonate to the natural harmony and life force within our cells. He states, "Because all activity involves stress . . . the body will need to readjust back to a sense of normalcy, or homeostasis, of balance. In other words, *the body seeks to get in 'harmony with itself* ."[5] With his kind of music or with chants and meditation tones and with TRT, you will be giving yourself a bath of "Light" and indeed, an incredible experience as well as being a highly efficient, relatively low-cost, and extremely practical method of releasing negativity from your entire being rather than storing it in your system for weeks, even years, resulting in premature degeneration, aging, chronic and terminal illness, and constant fatigue. A vacation once a year for relaxing and resting is not sufficient for adequate releasing of distress caused by the extraordinary pace of our daily lives, by old emotional patterns stored deep within, perhaps from childhood, by rigid, narrow thinking, and by spiritual feelings of inner emptiness and futility.

One of the hallmarks of wholistic health and living is the tenet that *you* assume responsibility for your wellness and wholeness. The truth is that it is not up to someone else to keep you well, nor is personal lack of wellness and wholeness always someone else's fault. Using TRT gives you an opportunity to assume this responsibility, privately, in your way, according to your own needs, as well as in conjunction with family and friends.

Health, wellness, and wholeness require the integrating of body, emotions, mind, and spirit Dr. Harold Bloomfield reminds us that "positive wellness rather than the mere absence of symptoms must be the goal of health care."[6] In TRT Seminars, I express it this way: "Remember always that health and wholeness are your divine birthright, which you have the *right* to claim now." The Radiance Technique provides a direct, natural, and harmless source of transmuting energy in your personal, unfolding process of life. TRT can be used by individuals of all ages to deal with distress and to promote positive stress responses. By using TRT daily, you are acknowledging your own involvement and direct participation in your healing or wholing process. With ongoing use of TRT, you are activating in a new, efficient way your power within for releasing negative stress accumulations, for balancing and renewing your energy and vitality, and for maintaining your health and wholeness.

For further information, please read *The Radiance Technique® On The Job*, by Fred W. Wright Jr., © 1992 Radiance Associates. This Expanded Edition includes the compilation of over 130 sharings from workers in varied professions who use TRT on-the-job around the globe! See Addresses page for specifics.

11

Cancer and
The Radiance Technique®

It is a particularly sad course of events, that many times those people who most steadfastly and responsibly attempt to live up to cultural rules develop the most serious illnesses. The literature is replete with examples characterizing cancer patients in general as "too good to be true"–people who are kind, considerate, unselfish and pleasant in the face of all adversity. . . . Individuals who begin to accept responsibility for influencing the state of their health deserve the greatest of congratulations.
**Carl and Stephanie Simonton
and James Creighton**

In The Radiance Technique seminars one of the most frequently asked questions is, "How can TRT help with cancer?" Many of those who take the TRT Seminar do so because either they or someone close to them is dealing with some form of cancer.

The Radiance Technique can be helpful in significant ways in the healing or wholing process of cancer patients. One of the

72

most common problems with cancer and with techniques such as chemotherapy, radiation, and surgery is the energy-draining, loss-of-vitality effect on cancer patients. In many cases, the person must select one or more of these current cancer-treating techniques even though the side effects can be devastating and healing results are not certain. TRT can be used effectively with whatever therapies the person is undergoing. TRT gives an immediate, direct, amplified contact with natural, vital Light-energy. Using TRT does not interfere with the traditional medical approaches, but it can give the patient an often greatly needed source of natural energy for restoring energy loss, for reducing stress, and for promoting the healing process.

TRT is also highly effective in dealing with the extreme physical pain often associated with cancer. In addition, TRT helps the cancer patient deal with emotional responses such as fear, depression, and anger. Many cancer patients who have studied TRT have found this source of Light-energy to be spiritually uplifting and to be an essential tool in helping to prepare for the dying process in so-called "terminal" situations.

One of the most profound and enlightening experiences I have had with TRT and with a cancer patient began several years ago in a northern city. After hearing the introductory lecture on TRT, a woman who appeared to be in her early fifties approached the speaker's podium. She explained that several years earlier she had battled with cancer, had won a reprieve, but now was suffering from a recurrence of the disease. Medical examinations revealed that the cancer had spread throughout her entire lympathic system, had invaded her brain, and had spread into her bone marrow. She had been diagnosed as being terminal and had been given only a few months to live. She explained further that she had tried a large number of healing techniques in addition to the chemotherapy and radiation. As she put it, "I have gone from A to Z to try to discover why I am dying of cancer and to find techniques appropriate in my healing process. I have even tried past-life regression to find the causes, but I still do not understand 'why'." Then she looked at me with intense, piercing eyes and in a challenging tone asked me what TRT could do for her. I held her gaze momentarily, looking deep within her, and responded, "TRT will help you with your pain." She admitted that she had been disillusioned with many techniques. She left the lecture without committing herself to take the seminar. The next morning she came with a friend to take the seminar. During the break, Janet shared with me that her physical pain was so intense that she was taking eight to ten prescription pain pills a day. She was angry, she said, because she was even missing her own dying process because the pain pills blurred and dulled her mind.

After the first activating energy transmission, Janet's face took on a new radiance. Her eyes began to sparkle and her facial skin, which had been dull and gray, was restored to color and brightness. In the seminar, we discussed the dying process and the importance of being in tune with the experience. She began to see a new dimension and to accept herself in a "new light." Later that week, she called to tell me that, after only five days of using TRT, she was taking only two to four pain pills a day. She was amazed at how clear her mind was and how much vital energy was being restored to her extremely drained body. She had been using TRT on herself at least three times a day, and other friends who had taken the seminar were also giving her hands-on sessions.

As the weeks passed, Janet was able to reduce her need for pain pills to only one every several days. A few months later, I saw her again. She had changed dramatically. Her face was radiant, her energy level was high, she had gained some weight, her self-confidence was restored, and she had begun teaching her beloved yoga classes again. Janet was a giver and a healer, and with TRT she was once again able to teach and give. She was also most impressed with how daily use of TRT enhanced the mental imagery technique she had learned at Dr. Carl Simonton's clinic, which specializes in cancer research. In addition to the medical therapies, she considered The Radiance Technique and the Simonton mental imagery to be her most effective daily tools.

Janet attended my next lecture in her area and shared with the audience how much the *quality* of her life had changed with TRT, how effective this technique was in pain relief but, most of all, how much spiritual inspiration and enlightenment she had received from her daily use and interaction with TRT sessions and meditations.

For the next two years she kept in touch with me by telephone and by mail. Once she wrote that her doctor felt that something was being "reactivated," possibly in her brain. Since she had been using TRT, she had grown substantial amounts of her hair on her head. Her self-confidence in her appearance was restored, and her embarrassment at her baldness caused by the chemotherapy, radiation, and other drugs was diminished. She also said that she was glad to have taken The Second Degree of TRT because "it gives me much satisfaction to do distant healing . . . it is a good feeling to me to think that I have at least tried to be of help to others."

Then word came that Janet had died—had made her transition from this life. Right to her last days on this plane, she had taught yoga and had lived a full and active life for nearly three years beyond what had been medically predicted. With TRT, she had been able to dissipate her extreme depression. Most important, however, she had continued to learn, to grow, and to undergo profound physical, emotional, mental, and spiritual transformations. In the last months, she wrote to me, "I believe that I am doing as well as I am because of TRT."

Janet had brought a wholistic approach into her consciousness and had reaped many benefits. She felt that the most important thing using TRT had given her was renewed vitality, a direct source for natural energy, and an inner strength and peace she had never before known. Indeed, her new light showed in her face, in her changed attitude, and in her determination to participate *actively and consciously* in this part of her own life process—wherever the journey was taking her. Her dying and death process was truly a beginning of a new cycle in her Continuum of Consciousness.

Janet's case has been discussed at length because it so clearly demonstrates the many levels of benefits possible from TRT for those persons dealing with cancer and with other extremely de-energizing diseases. In addition, her case raises the question, unanswered though it may be, whether she could have healed the cancer if she had been able to use TRT sooner. Too often, those who seek additional healing therapies do so in the terminal phase of the disease when even all the medical technologies have failed. When the alternative healing therapies

75

also appear to fail, these techniques are then unfairly crit-
icized, ridiculed, and dismissed as valueless. In this time of
expanded awareness, however, each of us has the opportunity
to perceive health matters from a larger perspective. This
perspective, wholistic in nature, includes the outstanding
advances of medical technology *as well as* other techniques
that promote health, well-being, and wholeness on all levels of
our being. With a wholistic perspective, you do not have to wait
until you are "terminal" on this plane of existence to explore
and use effectively wholeness-promoting techniques.

One of the most significant aspects of Janet's story is that
with daily use of TRT she became again an *active* participant in
her life process. She expressed to me that she no longer felt as
helpless and personally devastated by the cancer. Inwardly, she
grew, and the Light-energy accessed through TRT opened the
doors to deeper perceptions about her *process* and helped put
her in contact with other dimensions of her being.

An eighty-three-year-old woman who had undergone surgery to remove a cancerous lump from her intestines was given
the gift of a seminar in TRT by her concerned daughter. The
daughter, who held a Ph.D. in psychology, and her husband,
who was a practicing psychiatrist, had been benefiting from
use of this technique for nearly a year. Both were highly
impressed with the results of TRT on many levels. After surgery, her mother was getting chemotherapy weekly for approximately one year. At eighty-three, she had managed to keep a
bright attitude about life and was open to learning something
new. Accustomed to a high energy level all her life, she was
aware of the enormous energy drain she experienced after each
chemotherapy treatment. She also was apprehensive about the
side effects often related to chemotherapy such as loss of hair,
change in skin texture, and possible internal complications.
After the seminar, she gave herself daily hands-on sessions as
well as receiving sessions from her daughter. She immediately
noticed the positive change in her energy level with daily use of
TRT. Her face brightened, natural energy was restored where it
had been depleted, and her fears were alleviated. She was able
to release stress accumulated daily from taking care of herself
and helping her ailing husband. After one year, she was taken

off of chemotherapy, free of cancer. She still uses TRT for restoring energy, for reducing stress and for emotional balancing. In addition, she suffered no loss of hair and no other visible side effects from the chemotherapy.

At the Center in Atlanta and in my travels, I have worked with many women of all ages who are suffering from breast cancer. A woman in Detroit in her late twenties had undergone a radical mastectomy. Tests revealed that the cancer had spread to her lymphatic system, and the doctors were not optimistic in their assessment of the situation. She came to a TRT seminar depressed, frightened, and extremely weak physically. She was on a regular program of radiation, and with two young children at home she was losing energy faster than it was being restored. With the first activating energy attunement of TRT, her energy level increased dramatically. Others in the class could see the change in her energy right away. The heavy negativity surrounding her began to lighten. By the end of this first session, her cheeks were glowing and her eyes were shining.

During the next several days, we did group hands-on sessions during the seminar. In a private session on the fourth day, she revealed how many transformations she had gone through just being in the class and then by doing three to five hours of hands-on herself each day. The swelling and pain in her arm had been reduced greatly. She was beginning to think more clearly about ways to help herself and to promote healing. She said she was still terrified of death, but, when she was using TRT, her fears diminished. She said she had seen "white Light" being transmitted in each of the four Attunements of The First Degree of TRT. She knew the road ahead would be difficult and many things were yet unresolved within her, but through use of TRT her energy and her self-confidence had been restored and her pain released both physically and emotionally. She felt she was on a new cycle!

Since that time, I have received letters from her telling about her continued use of TRT, as instructed, and giving thanks for the opportunity to take this seminar. She believes she *is healed*, even though she has a long way to go, and TRT was an essential ingredient in this healing process.

Another woman, in her sixties, rapidly developed a cancerous tumor in her left breast. She reported that her oncologist explained the critical nature of the situation. They agreed on surgery within a few days. She wrote to me, "My physician son soon contacted an Authorized Instructor of The Radiance Technique in our city. She reacted instantly by directing to me this Radiant healing energy, which raised my energy, stabilized the emotions of my family and me, along with the added plus of peace of mind and heart during the various stages of preparation . . . my children, physician and wife, who had studied TRT together with a TRT Instructor (from the Center in Atlanta), gave me personal daily benefits."

At that time, my own schedule took me out of Atlanta. When I returned, I went to Emory hospital to give her a hands-on session. The surgery had been done on the previous Tuesday. The entire breast had been removed as well as the node under her arm. To everyone's relief, the tests indicated no apparent spreading of the cancer. To everyone's surprise, the scar was healing *without* discoloration and without swelling. Her arm lacked even the usual puffiness associated with this surgery. With daily use of TRT, her healing process had been accelerated. Her attending physician was very impressed with the results. She was released from the hospital after only five days instead of the usual ten. She returned to work within only one month. She said that her "energy buildup was unbelievable." A month later, both she and her husband took a TRT seminar so that they could do TRT for themselves and for each other. She wrote, "How blessed are those who have (1) received the benefits of TRT and (2) taken the next step—participation by preparation and using this technique in their lives daily."

Three years ago, a very frightened, desperate-sounding woman phoned me about the possibility of using TRT to help with a severe cancerous disease that was recurring across her nose and cheeks. She had been advised by expert physicians at Emory University that the necessary surgery would be extremely painful and slow to heal. This extensive and complicated surgery was scheduled for three months from the time she called. I immediately taught her TRT as well as giving her regular sessions three times a week. She used the hands-on of

TRT on her face *many* hours each day—even at work she would sit with her hands cupping her face to get extra radiance to revitalize and to release stress. She was truly surprised at the emotional and mental stability and peace of mind she was experiencing with use of TRT. Two months later, she went to Emory for testing relating to the upcoming surgery. The doctors were amazed at the transformation in her condition. She was rescheduled for less severe surgery from which she recovered more rapidly than had been expected. When I last heard from her, she said that she was using TRT to transform some old, negative emotional patterns. She also said that without the Light-energy accessed by TRT her surgery would have been a much worse ordeal.

Recently, a twenty-six-year-old woman with advanced cancer of the stomach and lungs took a TRT seminar. She came in physically weak and exhausted and emotionally depressed. She was having a great deal of difficulty dealing with her physical disease, with her energy depletion, with her three young children, with her marriage relationship, and with a full-time job. She told the class that she had been healthy and highly energetic all of her life, but the cancer had appeared suddenly and in an advanced stage.

She had almost completely given up any hope of living. She was deeply depressed and angered at her predicament. Since her usual energy level had been high, she could not believe how totally drained she felt after chemotherapy. With the first activating energy transmission of TRT, she could feel the natural energy flowing into her body. Her face brightened and her spirit elevated. During the last class, she told everyone that she managed to get in three to five hours of using TRT each day! As she put it, "I am a new person as far as my restored energy is concerned. I have a long way to go, but I feel so much less helpless with TRT—I don't even resent the chemotherapy as much since I can use TRT hands-on while receiving it."

The next account is of an incredible woman in her late forties who had worked both as a legal secretary and as a healer. She had studied and taught various forms of healing for nearly fifteen years. She began studying TRT, taking both The First and The Second Degree, and offered her services to others as a

79

therapist of TRT. Then, in the summer of 1980, she noticed a persistent sore throat and a small lump in the right side of her neck. Using TRT took away the extreme soreness, but the lump had not subsided. She decided to use alternate methods for healing, but by mid-fall the lump had gotten larger and harder.

In October, I saw her and recommended that she go immediately to a medical doctor who was a close friend of mine and who combined medical techniques with other wholistic methods. He had also taken The Radiance Technique seminar and was familiar with the ways she could help with her own healing process. After a thorough examination, he sent her to a surgeon, and surgery was scheduled for December. During surgery, however, only the right tonsil could be removed. The lump was determined to be malignant. She was scheduled for eight weeks of radiation followed by surgery to remove the lump.

She had radiation treatments five days a week for eight weeks. In her words, "Another amazing experience awaited me! Radiation is fire. Radiation destroys. I began immediately using TRT as a protection method, in addition to its healing energies, to transmute the fire of the radiation." At the same time, a team of others who had studied The Second Degree of The Radiance Technique, with skills in distance directing of this universal energy, transmitted healing energies to her twice a day.

The radiation treatments severely burned her throat. She could not eat, she rapidly lost forty-five pounds, and she lost enormous amounts of energy daily. As she later wrote, "And this was with use of TRT! I can't imagine what it would have been like without this technique. All I can judge by are the comments of the nurses and doctors made during my treatments and afterwards, and seeing other patients having similar treatment. They were worse off than I. At one point, I was told that very few people can complete the treatments without a break. I did. Thank God for The Radiance Technique!"

Before the next surgery, she came to the Center in Atlanta for nine days. Several of us devoted many hours day and night to giving her extended hands-on sessions of TRT. She wrote later, "They were so caring, so loving, so kind and helpful. . . . I went home uplifted and confident. They helped me to survive."

The final surgery was successful—the tumor had been totally encapsulated without spreading. In the hospital, she used TRT daily herself and could feel the vital energy being restored into her depleted being. In addition, a close friend, who had also studied TRT, gave her daily sessions in the hospital. The doctors and nurses were surprised at the rate of her recovery, and she was released ahead of schedule.

In telephone conversations with my friend, the wholistic medical doctor, he warned that for full recovery she would need to change many old patterns, be more aware of nutrition, and use TRT a great deal! The name of the game for cancer patients is restoring and conserving *energy*.

One year later I saw her again. The healing and wholing process was wonderfully evident. She had continued doing a great deal of TRT on a daily basis *and* had managed to change some old, limiting, unhealthy patterns. She and her husband had even moved to another state! Recently, she wrote to me about her experiences. She had used several approaches to healing and feels that they all have "their place in the universe." She had realized that "TRT touches every level and works in conjunction with all approaches—assisting, enhancing and perfecting the energies of each of them." At her last visit to her surgeon, late in 1981, he expressed surprise and pleasure at her appearance and good health. As far as he could tell by examination, she is free of the cancer. There is nearly no evidence of the surgery—almost no scarring is visible on her neck. With the skill and expertise of the surgeon and the Light-energy accessed by TRT restoring and balancing vital energy, she is on a new cycle of growth and transformation. She feels that she would "not be alive, well and whole today" if she had not had use of TRT.

What causes cancer? Why do some people get cancer while others do not? "Why me?" "What did I do wrong?" No one has simple, easy answers to these questions. Medical researchers continue to seek causes and solutions. Modern medical technology continues to offer treatments in line with the extent of its current but limited knowledge.

Cancer research suggests that cancer has many causes that could combine to result in the malignant cells. Carcinogenic substances, genetic predisposition, polluted air, water, and food supplies, radiation, and emotion-mental factors have all been related to cancer. Scientific researchers, however, have difficulty concluding unequivocally that any one of these factors is the only cause of cancer.

Regardless of the controversy, scientific research, and speculation about the causes of cancer, the person who is *experiencing* this illness must find ways of treating and dealing with it. From a wholistic perspective, a person can combine several therapies to promote the healing process and can become a responsible participant in this process. Perhaps the most significant benefit of TRT to cancer patients is in the simple, direct, easy-to-learn method, which allows the person to participate in restoring health. When faced with serious illnesses, a person often feels helpless and powerless. TRT gives the opportunity for an individual to become directly involved in the healing process. TRT helps to minimize or eliminate completely this sense of helplessness or powerlessness. With constant use of TRT, self-confidence is restored.

In the cases discussed in this section, one significant point was that each of those persons, at some point in dealing with illness, *decided* to become actively involved in the life process that was happening to him or her.

Medical therapies were successfully combined with The Radiance Technique. The benefits of using this technique were especially noted in restoring depleted vital energy, enhancing the other therapies, and releasing emotional-mental stress. Death is not a disease, and, in the case of the person who went through the dying process, TRT provided a vital source of confidence, inner strength, new insights, and peace of mind.

12

Pets, Plants and
The Radiance Technique®

All living things—both plant and animal—are linked in an extraordinarily designed, ecological balance. Man has an essential role to play in this chain of regeneration.
R. Buckminster Fuller

The Radiance Technique accesses vital, universal life energy and therefore can be used effectively on anything that is *alive*! Animals and plants are an integral part of our planetary system, and their destiny is linked with ours. Certain species of animals and plants are becoming extinct because mankind in modern societies has forgotten his *connection* with other living creatures. In our journey toward wholeness, we will all have to learn to share this planet with the native animals and plants who not only have the right to be here but also are a vital, integral part of our entire ecological system. Animals and plants exhibit an awareness different from ours, yet they share with us intelligence, natural growth cycles, health, disease, and death. Different does not mean inferior!

In the area of health and disease, animals and plants are affected as are human beings by the ravages of polluted air, water, and food sources. Because of their close contact with humans, domesticated pets share to an even greater degree the maladies currently arising in contemporary life. In recent times, pets have increasingly incurred diseases similar to ours. Motorized vehicles are constant sources of accidents and death for our pets. Pet psychologists have appeared on the scene to help when pets display emotional disorders from close contact with distressed human beings. Recently, *Time* magazine did an article on the use of massage therapy for pets suffering from physical stress caused by the pressures and rigors of modern life. *New Age* magazine featured a story on chiropractic techniques for animals. Of all the books available on wholistic health and natural healing, few offer a separate chapter on animals and pets. This book does. The Radiance Technique can be used with your pets and plants harmlessly. Let me share a few of the many experiences I have on record of using TRT to help pets, nondomesticated animals, and plants.

A user of TRT in Atlanta received a call from a local veterinarian to assist him with his own dog. His four-year-old female Great Dane had jumped a barbed-wire fence, missed, and mutilated the entire undersection of her body. He had operated on his dog twice in an attempt to get the skin and wounds to heal but to no avail. He was attempting one more operation to remove the massive amounts of dead skin. At this point, a student of TRT from the Center in Atlanta began giving the dog daily sessions before and after the surgery in a series of five hands-on sessions averaging thirty to forty-five minutes each. Within this small amount of time, the Great Dane healed beautifully. The veterinarian was grateful for discovering TRT and believed its universal energy saved his dog's life.

A five-year-old male Schnauzer named Erich, belonging to a friend of mine, suddenly contracted the devastating parvo disease. His owner had been gone all day and had returned home late in the evening. She noticed the dog was listless and not hungry. A couple of hours later, she discovered large amounts of dried blood that he had vomited. Realizing that he was severely ill, she took his temperature and found it was nearly 106 degrees. He was extremely dehydrated from diarrhea, and his body was ice cold. She rushed him to the veterinarian at

11:30 p.m. In the car, a friend gave Erich hands-on of TRT all the way to the office, and his icy skin became lukewarm. The doctor gave the dog an appropriate injection but told my friend that it was doubtful the dog would survive the night.

After returning home, she called several people who were trained in The Second Degree of TRT, which includes a highly efficient method for distance directing of radiant energy. They agreed to help by sending Erich healing energy. By the next morning the dog had improved but still was not "out of the woods." Another friend, trained in TRT, volunteered to go to the clinic and to administer complete hands-on sessions on Erich. The veterinarian was open to any help offered. In just two days, the dog had almost totally recovered and, to the amazement of all, including his doctor, Erich was eating normally and regaining energy and strength. To verify the disease, a blood test was taken. The test showed a positive reading—it was parvo. The dog had made a remarkable recovery in an unheard-of short time from a perilous, frequently fatal, disease.

Erich's TRT hands-on sessions continued on a daily basis, sometimes twice a day, to restore his energy level and eliminate all the effects of the devastating disease. Use of this technique literally had saved his life. It is important to note that the dog had been receiving hands-on sessions from its owner for nearly three years before this episode. During these years, she had found TRT to be an extremely effective preventive technique for all her pets, including two cats. Her vet bills were low, and her pets were maintaining high levels of positive health. When parvo hit her dog, his pre-existing positive health level and life-energy reservoir from the TRT sessions diminished the overall impact.

Now for the dramatic story of Buckwheat, who has become known as the "miracle dog of Atlanta," as told by his owner in edited form. Late one evening in June, eight-year-old Buckwheat sat on the patio watching over his backyard domain. He had shared a late-night piece of cake with his owners. Suddenly, two large dogs jumped the fence and attacked the friendly, easy-going hound dog. In the ensuing battle, his neck was nearly broken, his ears torn, his throat bitten, and he suffered severe liver damage. When his owners found him, he was in shock, dazed, disoriented, and near death. The veterinarian did all that he could, but Buckwheat did not respond well. He was losing vitality daily.

In July, a friend who had studied TRT came to see him. Lynn knew immediately that he needed more help than the medication and nursing care were providing. She gave the hands-on session of TRT to Buckwheat for an hour.

Days went by, and Buckwheat continued to get worse. His muscles were degenerating, the saliva glands were not functioning, and his weight dropped from thirty to fifteen pounds. The veterinarian concluded that his liver was damaged beyond repair and, regretfully, recommended that the dog be put to sleep. Lynn was informed of the situation and thereupon began a series of intensive hands-on sessions on Buckwheat. In addition, when she went home at night she used the distance directing method of The Second Degree of TRT with him. Lynn felt that, through TRT, she was able to feel intuitively the dog's vital energy level as well as his will to live.

With all the sessions he was receiving, his energy level increased, he regained use of his neck, ate well, and actually barked—the healing process had begun. It was "uphill" from that moment on. Now that he could finally eat, his diet was enriched with whole grains, fresh vegetables, meat, and eggs and always more of TRT! Several weeks later the vet examined him again and could not believe it was the same dog—even Buckwheat's liver *appeared to have regenerated itself*. The vet actually thought he was another hound dog. But the scars and torn ears, though healed now, validated Buckwheat's miraculous recovery.

I have not yet had the honor of meeting Buckwheat, but his gracious owner studied advanced levels of TRT for Buckwheat, for herself, and for her husband! She told the class of Buckwheat's "special radiance tale" and assured us that "his upset emotions and trauma had disappeared and that he had completely recovered his sense of humor, his playfulness, charm, and friendliness." With ongoing use of TRT, Buckwheat has been restored to health, to wholeness, and to life.

Many people who have taken TRT Seminars have reported how effective its use has been in treating a wide variety of disorders of dogs and other pets. One man found TRT helpful in getting his German Shepherd through her epileptic attacks. One woman's sixteen-year-old poodle had been suffering from severe coughing attacks and excessive liquids in the lungs. She used TRT each day on her dog and, within a week, these symptoms had reduced significantly. One woman reported that she used the hands-on on her dog's head every day for only ten minutes, and his highly tense, volatile energy changed to normal. In one class, one woman called TRT a "pet lifesaver" in stopping bleeding. Hit by a car and badly bleeding from a leg wound, her dog lay dying in the street. She ran out and used TRT, which immediately stopped the bleeding. With the help of friends, she got him to the vet, who expressed amazement at what had happened. He affirmed that without use of TRT the dog would have bled to death before she could get him to help.

It has been my experience as well as that of many others that cats respond well to the universal energy of TRT. They seem to be able to "tune in" naturally and with ease to this life energy. I am a fond lover of cats. For twenty years I have always had at least two cats, sometimes as many as five, as regular members of my household. In addition, several others are always passing through. For years I have consistently given my cats the hands-on part of TRT. I have found that overall they are healthier, brighter, and less frequently sick. My vet bills are lower. When the cats have needed medical treatment, it has tended to be less costly, the recovery has been quicker, and the side effects have been lessened.

I had an interesting experience with a stray who took up residence at my front door until I admitted her into the family and named her Buffy. As it turned out, Buffy had cancer of the bladder in its advanced stage. But the TRT hands-on sessions I used with her helped her relax and seemed to help the pain. The side effects of the medications were so potent that after consulting with the vet, I finally took her off the high doses and relied solely on use of TRT. Buffy was a very lovely cat but a very sick one. Yet, with TRT, she was able to eat and maintain her weight. When additional internal complications arose, she made her transition. She had, however, given me the opportunity of sharing her inner light and of learning how to treat sick animals with TRT.

In Atlanta, I have done a considerable amount of healing work with cats. As a result, the Center there frequently got calls for help with cats. One of the diseases we often encountered was feline leukemia. It is a devastating disease that strikes a cat suddenly, draining it of its vital energy and almost certainly resulting in death. Because it is a highly contagious disease, the ill cat is treated in its home. Special precautions are taken with cleaning my skin and clothes to avoid spreading it to other cats as well as to my own when I return home.

Several years ago, I received a call from a dejected, extremely upset, and deeply saddened owner of a wonderful three-year-old Siamese cat named Sylvia. Misidentified as to gender early in kittenhood, Sylvia actually was a boy! He had severe feline leukemia and had been sent home by the vet with the gloomy prognosis that death could be expected shortly. His despondent owner had decided to seek additional help.

When I began doing TRT hands-on sessions with Sylvia, he was completely lacking in vital energy. He was near death and could barely eat, and his eyes were glazed over—he was in the dying process. I gave Sylvia TRT sessions nearly every day for the first few weeks. On the third day, he was perched in the window at my "usual" arrival time. With TRT, the connection between us had been easily opened. Thereafter, his owner reported that he always knew when I was coming and would wait in the window for my car.

When I began using TRT with Sylvia, there were places on his body where his fur had fallen off, and he had large bluish-colored sores on his head, neck, and shoulders. During the early part of this process, his condition appeared to get much worse. He could barely move, he was extremely dehydrated, the sores got bigger and bluer, and he lost more fur and much weight. In the natural healing process, diseases sometimes get worse before reversing. TRT promotes this *natural* process but often reverses the disease sooner and then moves in the direction of restoring health.

His owner was distraught at how horrible Sylvia looked. She kept checking with the vet, who reassured her that Sylvia could not be harmed and reminded her that his illness was terminal. I had added Sylvia's name to my distance healing list. As is my custom, I direct healing energies to everyone on the list, people and pets, each evening. I also asked Sylvia's owner to play a certain record for him several times each day using a wholistic approach to healing even with pets! With TRT as the primary direct source of Light energy, I sometimes use secondary sources–especially certain musical pieces.

The process we went through with Sylvia taught me many things that later opened dimensions of understanding in my healing work with others. One evening while I was directing healing using The Second Degree, I had the experience of becoming *one* with Sylvia. It was as though I was inside him. I could see and *feel* the disease. I could clearly see the Light-energy accessed by TRT inside that cat, and I could see it as fire burning the disease *out* of him. That insight helped explain the horrible blue sores and all the draining pus. Outwardly, Sylvia was a terrible mess of sores, pus, skin, and bones. Inwardly, he was being transformed. I could also see that the negative was being *transmuted* into positive energy–it was pure, White Light.

It was an incredible process to behold. I was deeply grateful for the opportunity to go through this experience with Sylvia. Since then, many people who have studied TRT have shared similar experiences with me. With TRT, you direct this Radi-ant, Light-energy and become a co-worker in the healing pro-cess. With TRT, you are *not* using your personal energy nor are you in any way controlling the outcome.

I worked with Sylvia for more than two months, sometimes daily, sometimes with distance directing of energy only. About midway in this process, he appeared to be ready to die at any moment. Then, suddenly, he accepted food, a light returned to his eyes, and, gradually, he began to regain strength and vital energy. He needed all of this radiant energy he could get! At that time, I was not an instructor of TRT and therefore could not teach this technique to Sylvia's owner. But I knew deep inside of my being that I would one day become one so that I could teach those close to a pet or loved one, family or friend, how to use this profound and harmless technique.

Meanwhile, Sylvia's vitality was restored completely. The laboratory reports indicated that the leukemia was no longer present. His new fur was thick, shiny, and beautiful. One day in early fall, I stopped by to give him another hands-on session. I knew when I saw this healthy, playful, very much *alive* Siamese cat that he would not need any more hands-on from me. In his own special way, Sylvia let me know that day that he was completely well. Usually, when I began his hands-on session, he would settle down and quietly let me proceed. That day, however, with twinkling eyes, he playfully chewed my fingers, rolled around, and brought me his toys to play "fetch." With loving energy, Sylvia let me know his healing process was completed! It was my last visit with him, but occasionally through the months his grateful owner called to let me know that Sylvia was fine!

People from all parts of the country have shared with me their experiences with TRT and cats. After receiving only the first of TRT attunements of The First Degree, one woman reported to the class that she had gone home and used TRT with her cat, who had been listless and not eating. Within minutes, while she was administering TRT, her cat threw up a strange-looking substance, then ate her dinner, drank some water, and returned to normal. I instructed her to continue using TRT with her cat for several days to balance her energy and restore *ki* to a normal level. She did, with positive results.

One man reported that his six-year-old cat had suffered a broken leg in an unusual fall. The leg, though set properly by the vet, was not healing as it should have. I recommended that he give the cat thirty minutes of the hands-on of TRT each day, which he did. Within five days, the improvement was so enormous that the cat was going outside dragging its cast and leg. Previously, he had stayed in a corner, listless and depressed.

A woman in Minnesota said that she had taken in a stray cat who had been severely mistreated and then deserted by her owners. The cat had suffered severe emotional damage. She was afraid of people but had become aggressive rather than passive in her behavior. She would attack and bite people—even guests who came into her new owner's home. The hostile behavior continued for several years. Then her owner studied TRT, both The First and The Second Degrees. She then used it with her cat on a regular basis for several months. When at work during the day, she was able to direct radiance at a distance to her cat. Within four months, the improvement in the cat's personality was noticed by all who knew her. She began relating to people without inflicting scratches and bites. TRT had touched the nonphysical level of her cat-being that had been bruised and battered. Her owner has kept me updated on her cat's continued progress. She reports that the cat "seems to enjoy life more now. She is less tense and now hardly ever exhibits her old, 'spooky,' jumpy, scared self." With use of TRT, her healing is in progress, and she is gaining wholeness in her cat-life experience.

Sometimes in our lives, each of us might have the opportunity to help animals other than our pets. In each of the cases I am about to describe the opportunity came to me unexpectedly. I was thankful to have the gift of TRT and to learn more about the animal kingdom that exists all around us.

I had attended a soccer game in Tampa, Florida, and had been impressed by the vigor of the Rowdies, by the incredible spirit of the crowd, and by the joyful array of colors filling the stadium. Upon leaving the game, we were sitting in the midst of a traffic jam when off to my right I saw something move in the grass near the curb. Since traffic was stopped, I got out and carefully approached what turned out to be a seagull, no doubt one of Jonathan Livingston's relatives, with a badly broken wing. It appeared that the bird had been hit by a car and abandoned. Having had no previous experience with injured, undomesticated animals, I stood there for a moment wondering what to do. The seagull could not be left there. He could not fly, he could no longer fend for himself, and he would not survive. Remembering how effective I had found TRT to be in calming people, I took a deep breath, stepped forward, and reached out for the seagull with radiance in my hands. He fluttered and stumbled a few feet. I stopped—he stopped. I proceeded toward him again, picked him up, and got into the car. Immediately, I could feel this radiant energy pouring from my hands into his entire body. I have always loved seagulls but had never touched one and had never held one in my hands. I could hardly believe this was happening. It was an incredible experience. Without TRT, I know that I would not have had the confidence to touch that seagull.

With the hands-on of TRT, he calmed down and absorbed the vital energy. The seagull seemed somehow, to know what this Universal energy was–he seemed to know instinctively that it was harmless, healing, life-force energy. He seemed to absorb it with his whole being. I was vividly aware that the energy flowing through that seagull was the same energy flowing through me. The contact was there. He never once tried to bite me even though I did not have his beak covered. We drove from Tampa straight to the Suncoast Seabird Sanctuary in Indian Rocks Beach on the Gulf, north of St. Petersburg, Florida.

It was after midnight, dark, and cold but, after we had rung the bell several times, a sleepy but kind, gentle, elderly man admitted the seagull for treatment. I went to visit him the next morning. He was doing remarkably well after surgery. He had lost a wing, but he could still live a useful seagull-life, taking care of himself and doing his part in the ecological system. I had learned a new dimension of using this profound technique and, through it, had learned a great deal about the expression of the life-force energy on this planet.

About a year later, while I was walking along the seashore, I came upon a cormorant twisting around dizzily in the sand. I called to a friend for help. Using the TRT hands-on, we managed to get the bird calmed. We used a towel over his long, active beak to avoid bites. Holding the cormorant in my lap, I began using TRT with this beautiful aquatic creature of nature. We went straight to the Suncoast Seabird Sanctuary, where it was determined that the cormorant had been a victim of poisoning, probably from polluted water or food. This cormorant could, however, be saved with antibiotics. We both continued doing TRT distance directing of radiant energy on this bird until it was released from the sanctuary.

Not long ago, I came across another lovely cormorant on the beach who was also in trouble. Somehow the bird's left leg had been so badly broken that it could not fly or move very far. Realizing that the bird was too alert for me to handle without proper equipment, two of us trained in TRT began directing this energy to it. We could only get within a couple of feet of him. Once again, I drove to the Suncoast Seabird Sanctuary for help. Earlier that day, staff from that sanctuary had tried to catch this cormorant but the bird had gotten into the water and avoided the net. With the TRT Light-energy in contact with the bird, I knew he was ready to be helped.

Through TRT a direct connection of healing, radiant energy had been provided, letting him know that it was safe to accept help. He was calmer and more trusting now. This time, a friend and I used TRT without touching the bird physically, and he was captured and treated. His leg healed and soon he was set free. TRT was an essential tool for use in helping this beautiful but severely injured bird. Without such an effective technique, I might have been just another person passing by the bird, sympathetic to its plight but not knowing what to do.

Modern scientific research has given us much information about plant sensitivity and plant awareness. Caring for household and garden plants is a rewarding though serious endeavor. We have evidence that plants respond to our love and caring attention and that they shrink from attacks by people and pets. Accessing universal, Light-energy, TRT is a highly effective tool for use in working with plants.

One woman shared her exciting experience with growing a summer vegetable garden and using TRT. She reported, "I held each seed in my hands pouring radiance into them. I seemed to be able to sense the life-force energy within the seeds in connection with use of TRT coming from my hands. When the seeds began sprouting, I would carefully cup my hands around the small plants for several minutes. In the process of using TRT with my vegetables several times a week, I myself experienced a deep sense of inner peace. I felt as though I had been one with the natural growth cycle. I was much less tense and more centered than I had ever been in my life. I was also doing the hands-on session with myself early each morning. The beautiful, full, large vegetables my family and I ate all summer were the reward of my efforts. My friends and family were amazed at my gardening success that summer in contrast to my previous failures. There is simply no doubt in my mind that using TRT was the ingredient responsible for such abundance."

Now for the famous rubber plant story of Atlanta. During the second session of a seminar, a woman brought in a pathetic, nearly dead rubber plant. She had gotten it for twenty-eight cents at a local K-Mart. With barely a spark of life in it, the little plant was green-brown and sagging in its pot. In the previous class, I had discussed the use of TRT with all living things, including plants. But I will have to admit that when I saw her bringing in that more than half-dead plant, I myself had a moment of hesitation. I took a deep breath, continued the seminar, and directed radiant energy to the plant for all I was worth!

Others in the class helped by using the hands-on of TRT from its roots up, which is the best place to begin. The vital, radiant energy can then be carried upward and distributed. Several months later I had occasion to talk with this woman and, tentatively, I asked her about the plant. With enthusiasm, she responded that it had grown incredibly! She had taken it to her office and often put it under her desk to direct this radiant energy to it between her feet all day. Everyone in the office had watched in amazement as it got bigger and bigger. Pieces had been cut, and additional offspring of this gigantic plant had been given away. The story of this once nearly dead rubber plant with its "healing" through TRT became "widely" known! There is no doubt that with TRT this plant had progressed in its natural evolution to wholeness and, in the process, its story had touched all of us deeply.

Many people have reported similar experiences with TRT and their plants. One man wrote of his success in growing roses using TRT; another told of the healing and re-energizing of his favorite willow tree. A woman in Florida shared her experience of using TRT distance directing of energy with her delicate flower bushes and citrus trees during the hard freeze in 1980. By spring, her yard was in full array, lush with budding life. Her neighbors, who had lost their plants, were amazed at the abundance of her yard. Hers was the only living, green back-yard on the block!

The purpose of this chapter has been to share some experiences about how effective TRT has been with pets, other animals, and plants. There are many additional ways TRT could be used in this context. One of the unique aspects of TRT is that it provides a connection for vital, Light-energy, which can be used creatively, efficiently, and harmlessly, and adapted to any situation by the person with the "touch of radiance."

For further information, please read *The Radiance Technique® and The Animal Kingdom*, by Marvelle Lightfields, ©
1992 Radiance Associates. This book includes selections from
hundreds of sharings by animal lovers all over the world, as
well as chapters on how to help your pets with TRT, support
endangered species, and expand with the death-and-dying process. See Addresses page for specifics.

13

Dying, Death and
The Radiance Technique®

*Right up until the moment of transition
one carries all the results of existence in
space and time within the essence and
the self. But at transformation, all of
that will be left behind. One enters the
new life without remnants of the past.*
Sufi, Al Wasi

One of the most important, significant, and profound things
you will ever do in this life is die. In fact, taken from an
expanded perspective, the two major events of your life are
your birth and death. Your birth marked a dramatic transition
from a previous energy state, whatever the form, into a "life" on
what we perceive as the physical plane. Just as profoundly,
your death is a process of making a transition from this physical form to that of another level of being. There is no proof that
consciousness is terminated at one's physical death on this
plane. In fact, quite the contrary appears to be true!

Throughout our history on this planet, since we first contem-
plated the extent and depth of our being, we have always
spoken and written of a reality existing beyond the limits of
this so-called physical plane. In modern times, the Swiss

96

psychiatrist Carl Jung said, "Nobody can say where man ends."[1] His statement reflects ancient man's assertion that there is a continuum of life and Consciousness even though the outer forms change.

More than five thousand years ago, the Egyptians affirmed their knowledge of the immortality of human Consciousness. In *The Book of the Dead*, which the Egyptians actually called the *Book of Coming Forth to Light*, many levels of the life of the soul were described, and it was written, "I am like the stars who know not weariness—I am upon the Boat of Millions of Years."[2]

The inner knowledge about life and science was kept secret and hidden, revealed to only a few chosen initiates. But in the current New Age of humanity, the doors are being thrown open and the knowledge distributed to all of us.

Attributed to Lao Tsu is the statement, "There is a reality prior to heaven and earth."[3] Plato wrote, "The body of heaven is visible, but the soul is invisible, and partakes of reason and harmony."[4] In the Middle Ages, St. Thomas Aquinas stated, "The soul exists independent of the body, and continues after the body dies, taking up a new spiritual body."[5] In the new physics, consciousness is associated with all the quantum mechanical processes. Eugene Wigner, American Nobel Prize winner, puts it this way, "The recognition that physical objects and spiritual values have a very similar kind of reality has contributed to my mental peace. It is the only known point of view which is consistent with quantum mechanics."[6] Sir Arthur Eddington commented, "It is a primitive form of thought that things either exist or do not exist."[7] To this rich tradition Elisabeth Kubler-Ross adds, "I am convinced that there is life after death . . . death does not really exist."[8]

In all of human history, no culture has tended to treat the dying in such an antiseptic, non-involved manner as we do. In our society, we treat the dying as though they were actually dying rather than being in the process of a transition and a birthing into another state of Being. Dying and death are an integral part of human life, setting the boundaries in which we can measure our life's meaning. Elisabeth Kubler-Ross wrote, "But if we can learn to view death from a different perspective, to reintroduce it into our lives so that it comes not as a dreaded stranger but as an expected companion to our life, then we can learn to live our lives with meaning—with full appreciation of our finiteness, of the limits of our time here."[9]

Death is not a disease. It is one of the most significant, dramatic, and meaningful acts of your life, completing a cycle of existence of this plane. Death is not a final termination of your being. Death is a beautiful natural process of integrating all that you have been into the always present and eternal moment of "Being Here Now." Death is the deep, full breath we take as we make our transition into the next phase of our unfolding process. In truth, it is a glorious moment of "birthing" ourselves into a new existence.

Dying and death are a process in which we are utterly and completely involved from the moment of our physical birth. In our modern society, we have been disconnected from our own source, we have been unplugged and separated from our life-sustaining line, and we have "forgotten" how to make that prime, essential contact with who we really are.

Continued attention has been given to the gains of the outer world with little regard for our inner being, and, as a group, we have fallen asleep and become unconscious to our "real connection." Dazzled by modern technologies and blinded by the sensationalism of outer forms, we have lost touch with our myths, true religion, rituals, and symbols, which carefully preserved and transmitted to us knowledge essential to our wholeness.

Somehow, dying in our culture has become not only unspeakable but also unthinkable! It is not polite. In our society today, it has become the "supreme taboo." We tend to consider dying as the "worst thing" that can possibly happen to us. Yet dying is a completely natural, fulfilling, culminating, and liberating experience—no matter when it comes to each of us. There is no tragic or untimely death. There is only that which is part of your total unfolding. All the pieces fit as a part of a larger whole. Indeed, no single piece could be cast aside once it has been set into motion. Without each part, the whole would not be what it is.

In my healing work with The Radiance Technique®, I have had many opportunities for growth and increased understanding of the nature of healing and wholing. Needless to say, the biggest challenges and most profound opportunities came when I was called in to try to "save someone from death." Let me share one of my early opportunities to use TRT in a terminal illness situation.

I was called by the family of a man in his early thirties who was dying of liver cancer. Having heard from a friend that I "had cured her tumor," Phil's wife and mother insisted that I was to come and perform a "miracle healing." After the phone call, I went into prayer and mediation. I knew that I had not *personally* cured their friend's tumor but rather had used TRT to transmit radiant, Light-energy to her. From the phone call, I was aware of the desperate, tense, and highly emotionally charged energy of Phil's wife and mother. Their demand for me "to do an instantaneous healing" left no doubt as to the degree of their expectations.

One of my most important early lessons in healing work, for which I am filled with deep gratitude, was that of letting go of ego in the healing process. The healer or the transmitter of Light-energy cannot let the outer self seek its own satisfaction or gratification in any way. Nor can your ego be attached to outer results and expectations.

When I arrived at the hospital, I met Phil, who was, as it turned out, in his very last stages of life on this plane. Because of heavy drug doses, he was not conscious then, nor did he ever regain consciousness. The cancer had spread from his liver and pancreas to his lungs and stomach. Additional complications had set in because of the extreme deterioration of his bodily functions. Because of his weakened and terminal state, the doctors had determined that surgery was not possible. His wife and mother were hysterical and in shock.

What happened in the following days gave me deep knowledge of TRT as a complete and profound technique for use in the dying and death process. TRT is the best tool I know of for someone to use in helping, supporting, and nurturing the body, mind, and soul of oneself or of another person in the dying process. In the last days of his life, I gave Phil many complete hands-on sessions of TRT, spending extra time on his liver and pancreas. During the night after the first session, he discharged enormous amounts of mucus from his lungs. From then on he could breathe more normally, whereas before he was gasping, struggling to breathe, and choking on the clogged mucus in his throat and lungs. The next morning the doctor was amazed at how much the extreme swelling in Phil's liver had been diminished. Color and radiance were already being restored to Phil's gray, pale face—he was resting peacefully, and he *was* going through his dying process.

During the next five days, I continued to give Phil complete hands-on sessions of TRT. In the early hours of the sixth day, Phil released from his body. It had been a deep honor to assist him in this beautiful process. Through the use of TRT, a direct line inwardly from me to him had been opened. This contact was directly in touch with his soul. It was an exquisite experience—one of pure ecstacy—it was beyond the limits of these words to describe! With the radiant, Light-energy, accessed by TRT, Phil had received immediate benefits on the physical plane in making him more comfortable for his death. Through TRT came also the experience of touching deeply into the Essence of his Being. I saw his Light and, silently within, I knew him, knew his struggles and his triumphs, knew his Light, was One with him, shared the entire magnificent process of dying with him, and was awed by its majesty. It changed his life, and it changed mine forever. The old fears, misunderstandings, and misinterpretations of death fell away, dissolving instantly into the cosmic Radiance of Forever.

The experience I had shared with him in the inner dimensions was one of Joy, one of fullness, one of celebration. It was as though a cosmic event of great significance was happening and all the stars were there—the Light was incredible! In the inner being, the entire process was powerful yet gentle, yang yet yin—filled with Radiance and Light. His inner peace was overwhelming.

And, in sharp contrast, the outer activities in the room around him seemed trivial, empty, and not real—the sterility of the hospital, the hesitancy of the staff, the fears and numb resignation of his mother, the mounting terror, anger, and bitterness of his wife. Everyone around him was caught up in the outer process—that of his body letting go of the life-force, the *ki*. In the outer form, it appeared to be somehow cold and final, but, *at the same time*, in the inner planes, a great event was taking place. The outer appearance was only an illusion. The truth was in the inner process. Through TRT, I had come in conscious contact with this truth—transforming my consciousness of death expanding in spirals of knowingness about this profound process.

In ancient Tibet and Egypt, instructions were given to the dying person on how to release the soul from the body and how to make the profound transition from one state of Being to another. Someone usually participated in the dying process, acting as a guide, a support system. Today we tend to avoid participation in the dying process. We often leave the dying alone, rationalizing our fears with: "Let him die in private," "Call me when it's over," or "She would prefer to be alone." TRT can be used as a support for bridging the gap from the ancient wisdom to the modern predicament. In many and varied situations since my early experience with Phil, I have been honored to share TRT with many individuals in the dying process. The Radiance Technique and its direct access to Radiant, Light-energy allows for contact with all levels of the person's Being and provides a safe, natural technique for supporting the releasing of energy from the body at death. The experience of death is no longer to be feared. Our daily lives can be lived with a new perspective, with a dynamic wholeness, and with an awareness of our own immortality. At the "Continuum" exhibition in Minneapolis, a deeply provocative question is posed: "If you were sure of your own immortality, would you live your life differently?" The experience of death is no longer to be feared. Our daily lives can be lived with a new perspective, with a dynamic wholeness and with an awareness of our own immortality.

In seminars, I instruct on how to use TRT to its fullest in helping a family member, a friend, or a patient in the process of dying and death. Many people have written to me through the years expressing how the use of TRT gave them the confidence to reach out and touch loved ones who were dying, how much they had learned in this process about death and ultimately about life, and how new insights into immortality had been gained.

One gentleman returned to a seminar to share his experience with TRT as a death and dying technique. He gave us this account. His father was hospitalized with terminal cancer. Tom was called to come immediately because death was expected any minute. From childhood, Tom's relationship with his father had been extremely difficult. As a sensitive, artistic child, Tom had withdrawn from his father's domineering "macho" mentality. Before he was ten, Tom had been taken by his mother to another city to live. Through the years, his only contacts with his father, though sparse, had been, at best, unpleasant. In addition, his father's alcoholism had been a "turn-off" for Tom. Through the years, he had continued to harbor bitter resentment, hostility, and hatred for his father.

Tom was in his mid-fifties now, but, when the phone call came demanding his immediate presence at his father's deathbed, the old angers exploded inside him. Reluctantly, he left for New York. As each step took him closer to his dying father, his tensions increased to a substantial anxiety level.

Outside his father's hospital room, Tom took a deep breath, opened the door, and came face to face with this man who had held such power over him emotionally and mentally through all these years. Here was his father, now broken, weak, pale, barely conscious, and nearly dead. The level of physical pain his father was experiencing was excruciating. He was barely able to speak to Tom.

Tom said that, in that moment, the only thing he could think of was to use TRT now. His father's pain was increased by the additional complications of severe arthritis and a difficult heart problem. He could only be given a limited amount of pain pills. His father's extreme pain had triggered compassion in Tom. He told us that the only thing that kept him from feeling completely helpless was being able to use TRT right then, in the immediate situation. Without TRT, he would have been a passive bystander, and he might even have avoided staying in his father's room.

As it turned out, his father asked him repeatedly to continue the hands-on session of TRT since he was experiencing great relief from his severe pain. Remarkably, his father's color was returning and his eyes were getting brighter. Tom noted that a

Radiance, a "Light-energy" began to emanate from his father's head instantaneously from contact with the Universal energy accessed by TRT.

By the end of the second day, his father was resting well, but the *ki* was vacating his physical form. Tom said they had devised a hand signal for his father to let him know when he wanted Tom to do a hands-on session of TRT. Talking consumed too much energy. Around noon of the third day, his father made his transition. Tom was holding his dying father's head while applying TRT. He then used TRT to attune his father's heart center to universal love. He told me that he could feel his own Oneness with his father's Essence—it was a warm and peaceful experience, filled with Love and Light. He said that with TRT he could "feel" his father's soul releasing from the physical form. Later, as Tom was leaving, he saw that the entire room was radiating with a magnificent White-Light-energy.

Tom had shared his experience with the class because he wanted others to know how important TRT had been as a dying and death technique. For one significant time in their lives, he and his father had shared an experience of love and peace on an inner, silent, and *real* level. He said that he knew there was much left inside him about his father that needed working out, but through using TRT in this process most of the doors previously sealed with negativity from the past had been opened.

There are no limits to how TRT can be used with any person or pet experiencing the process of dying. The momentous occasion of death represents a truly cosmic happening as the Soul continues on its journey into new dimensions. The Radiance Technique gives you a powerful yet gentle and harmless way of participating without intruding, of touching life, not death, and of experiencing Oneness, not separateness, with yourself or with another going through this profound process.

What a wonderful day it will be when nurses, doctors, and other professionals treating the dying are also trained using TRT. What a valuable technique for others, such as the Hospice groups, who work with the terminally ill. TRT can be easily incorporated into the conventional medical framework and into other health and well-being methods. What a beautiful expanding and transforming process opens to each of us when we use TRT as a Light-energy support for helping, guiding, nurturing, and supporting ourselves, our loved ones, our friends, and our fellow humans and our pets through the natural process of dying.

14

Instantaneous Healing With The Radiance Technique®

Energy can enter and leave space-time.
Dr. Jack Sarfatti

Throughout the history of mankind's journey on this planet, accounts of instantaneous healings are found again and again. It is true, indeed, that so far not everyone in every situation experiences instantaneous healing, but this phenomenon does exist not as a possibility but as a fact of human experience. As Eugene Wigner, American Nobel Prize winner, put it, "Every phenomenon is unexpected and most unlikely until it has been discovered. And some of them remain unreasonable for a long time after they have been discovered."[1]

What is instantaneous healing and what are some of the aspects of the mechanism involved? The dictionary defines *instantaneous* as "occurring or completed without delay."[2] A related word is *spontaneous*, which is defined as "happening or arising without apparent external cause; self-generated; voluntary and impulsive; unpremeditated."[3] In seminars, I generally employ the term "spontaneous healings" in reference to experiences in which healing or wholing occurs within a relatively short period of time with the use of TRT. Some people have also had instantaneous healings with TRT.

The essential mechanism underneath a spontaneous healing can be understood in the term "extempore" from the Latin *ex* meaning "out of" and *tempus* meaning "time." Spontaneous healings occur in that space which transcends the limits of the outer world and the outer self—the body, emotions, and mind. The person is *literally* "out of time" during this process. The person experiencing spontaneous healing is liberated for an instant, freed in a flash, released from the bondage of old patterns, and connected directly with the eternal, Universal life-force. There are no limits in that dimension.

Descriptions of instantaneous healings by people who have had the experience include several elements of similarity. For example, descriptions include seeing or becoming intense, pure "white Light," having no sense of time as we know it, oneness with God, freedom from fear, and transcending to a total awareness. This experience takes the individual out of the old patterns or limits and shifts him into another dimension of being. Sometimes such an experience occurs when one is in deep meditation or through creative imagery, and even in moments of intense crisis. With TRT, spontaneous healing can happen with direct use and focusing of this Light-energy. One of my clients who was bringing her eleven-year-old daughter for hands-on sessions of TRT for eczema arrived late. She and her daughter were visibly upset, and the three-month-old baby was still crying. As they were on their way to my office, a car had stopped suddenly in front of their car, and the baby had been hurled off the front seat, had banged his forehead on the dashboard, and had fallen to the floor. The bump on his head was severely swollen, bright red, and, from his yells, still painful. We all sat down, and I held the baby, using TRT directly on the bump. We all talked, and everyone began to relax. Immediately, the baby stopped crying, and within four minutes the swelling and the redness on his head had disappeared. His mother and sister were truly astonished. I suggested that they both take a TRT Seminar so that in the future *they* could use it in emergency situations as well as at other times.

A nurse in Detroit, who had taken TRT, works in an elementary school. A young girl stung by a bee was brought screaming into her office. The child's arm was swollen, red, and stinging.

106

The nurse sat her down in a chair and began using TRT hands-on while talking to the child. The nurse reported that within minutes the bee's stinger fell out of the wound, the swelling left, and the redness was gone. In addition, the child's usual allergic reactions to bee stings never happened. Both she and the child were amazed at this instantaneous healing. In a few more minutes, the little girl was dismissed and resumed her outdoor play.

Susan and her date were leaving a London theater. It was a rainy, cold night in January. Suddenly, she slipped down the stairs, hitting her knees with great force, tumbled across the sidewalk, and bumped into a street lamp. The pain in both her knees and in her head was excruciating. In a blurry moment, she remembered to use TRT. She sat there for a few minutes until the pain and swelling in her knees and head subsided. Then she got up, and the two went on with their evening. She said that without immediate use of TRT not only would she have been hurt for a longer time but also that her entire vacation in England would have been destroyed. She had no doubt about the severity of the injuries and the effectiveness of TRT "on the spot."

An attorney, Ken, who took the seminar to help a beloved niece through the terminal phase of a very difficult disease, reported during the second class session that his four-year-old son had fallen down the stairs to the backyard. He had heard the scream and dashed immediately to help the boy. The child had a large bump on his head and was crying uncontrollably. Ken held the child and used TRT on the bruise and on the back of his head. Within minutes, the bump and bruise were gone, and the boy was completely calm and went on to play. Ken noted that this experience was amazing for two main reasons: (1) the complete healing of the bump in just a few minutes and (2) the child's change to calmness. Ken said that his son had always been particularly frightened of any falls, large or small, and it usually took several hours to calm him down after such an experience. Ken had four other children and said he was glad to have TRT for future use and to save on medical bills!

One woman wrote that when she was cleaning a crystal chandelier, a 75-watt bulb, which had been burning for about five hours, touched her right upper arm. She realized it was burning but could not jump quickly because she was involved with replacing a heavy strand of crystal. She finally moved slowly off the chair and used TRT for only ten minutes. She said that "the deep crescent-shaped burn on her upper arm was gone—the spot never blistered, peeled, hurt, or discolored."

A woman in New York, who was in her sixties and was using TRT successfully to treat a severe, eighteen-year-old arthritis condition, wrote about her other benefits. One cold, windy, snowy morning, she had gotten up with the beginnings of a sinus cold. She wrote that "one ten-minute hands-on sessions and my sinuses were *normal*." She added at the end of the letter that the fee for the TRT Seminar was "a drop in the bucket, as they say—what you are teaching is priceless!"

A woman in her early thirties was scheduled for surgery on a large kidney stone that would not dissolve with medication. Carol and Larry, business associates of hers, gave her a forty-five-minute hands-on session of TRT and suggested that she have X-rays before surgery in case the stone had changed in any way. The next day she checked into the hospital and, after much difficulty, managed to get additional X-rays. To everyone's surprise, to the doctor's chagrin, and to her own relief, the kidney stone was gone. Her surgery was canceled. After a year, she reported no recurrence of the condition.

Twenty-three-year-old Jim worked as a welder in a sheet metal factory. His mother had given him a TRT seminar as a special Christmas gift. After the second session, he went to work. At the job, he reached for a piece of hot metal, picked it up, and realized he had on only one of his special gloves—his other hand was bare. Immediately, he felt pain. He dropped the hot metal, sat down, and immediately used TRT on his hand. He said he was afraid to move or to look at his hand—he just sat, bent over, applying hands-on. About thirty minutes later, he looked at his hand. The healing had been spontaneous! There was no swelling, no redness, no pain, and no blisters. The dirt that had been on his fingers was now clearly embedded in his skin. The skin on his hand was smooth and shiny as though it had been ironed. Everyone in the class examined his hand and realized that TRT had promoted an instantaneous healing. He said he did not know what he would have done without this technique. Later, his boss confirmed that the temperature on the metal at the time he moved it would have been 1,200 to 1,500 degrees–impossible to touch with a bare hand without severe, permanent damage.

On a tour of Egypt in 1980, one of the women tripped on a large cement block and fell heavily. She had not seen the block and did not have time to buffer the fall. She hit hard on the base of her tailbone. She said the immediate pain was excruciating and she lost consciousness. I was standing a few feet away, saw the accident, ran to her, and immediately used TRT on the base of her spine and the top of her head. Instantaneously, she regained consciousness, the pain dissolved, she stood up, and her recovery was complete. She said, "When you touched me I could see, somewhere in my being, the White-Light energy of radiance going up my spine. I could feel my legs, back and head being healed instantly." The entire process from her fall to her spontaneous healing took less than one minute.

A woman reported that her husband had come home badly frightened and with a neck injury from a car accident. Realizing that he was in a state of anxiety and shock, she stretched him out on the floor and gave him a hands-on session while he continued explaining what had happened. Instantly, the pain and swelling left his neck and, within ten minutes, he had completely relaxed. TRT had spontaneously balanced his energies emotionally and physically.

During another class, I was demonstrating the special hands-on session positions on a man in his late forties. While I was talking, I had kept my hand on the upper part of his spine. All of a sudden, we all heard a loud "pop." Surprised, I stopped in mid-sentence. The man I was using for demonstration said he had been healed instantly of a painful blocked energy spot where a vertebra had been out of place for several months and had resisted healing with other therapies. With TRT, there is no need to manipulate body parts–the radiant, Light-energy was enough to snap it back into place!

I was exiting an auditorium through two very large and very heavy wooden doors and caught a finger between the two doors as they closed shut with force! The pain was intense. The finger turned bright red and swelled immediately. I sat down outside and used TRT on it for fifteen minutes. The pain stopped instantaneously. When I looked at my finger, its color and size had returned to normal. I was amazed. Using TRT had spontaneously reversed the injury process! There was no trace of any damage to the finger.

On the third day of a class, a young mother, Karen, came into the room with obvious joy! She had been unsure of TRT but had taken the course to use it for herself in healing some difficult health problems. Karen told us her story. Her two young children had been wrestling in the living room and one accidentally tossed the other, who bumped his head on the corner of the TV. A large red bump swelled up across his entire forehead. Everyone panicked. His grandfather ran to get ice, his grandmother ran to get a wet cloth, and Karen immediately used TRT hands-on on his forehead amid his loud screaming. Instantly, the bump was gone. By then, the others had returned with all the various remedies. The little boy was laughing. They were all sold on TRT as they saw for themselves that there was no trace whatever of the previously severe bruise—no swelling, no redness, and no discoloration. Her son said, "Mommy, now you have magic hands!"

This boy's words reminded me of Arthur C. Clarke's famous "Third Law," which states, "Any sufficiently advanced technology is indistinguishable from magic." This idea reflects the process involved with TRT.

Many people frequently report to me instantaneous healings during one of the four Attunements of TRT First Degree given in that seminar. The descriptions are usually similar to one another. A woman in her fifties, who had been a psychic healer for twenty years, reported an instantaneous healing of a severe lower back injury during one of TRT Attunements. During this process, she said she felt intense warmth, saw "white Light," and felt the blocked energy release from her back. After twelve years, this injury was still causing severe pain and restricting her daily activities. Now she was free of it. When I saw her a year later, she confirmed that the spontaneous healing had been complete and that with daily use of TRT she was feeling better than ever as well as looking young and radiant!

During the first Attunement of TRT, Marilyn reported to the class that she felt her neck being healed instantaneously with an intensely warm energy. Three years previously she had been in a car accident that had severely injured her neck. She had tried various therapies, but nothing had released the pain and stiffness. During the next sessions, Marilyn was thrilled to show everyone how easily she could now turn her head from side to side.

Robert, a young man in his late twenties from Chicago, returned to one of my lectures two years after taking the TRT Seminar. He told the audience that, during the fourth activating attunement, he had experienced an emotional, instantaneous healing. He had been too shy to say anything to me. He also wanted to be sure it would last. He explained that he had seen a flash of white Light, had felt hot and cold at the same time, and had experienced a release of anger, anxiety, and fear that he had been storing for years. He knew that he had been healed emotionally. He also knew that he was now free of his extreme addiction to cigarettes. In the subsequent two years, he had never smoked again.

A man in his early fifties noticed that a chronically stiff shoulder healed spontaneously during an Attunement Process. He reported to the class that he saw a flash of white Light, felt a deep warmth, and felt the energy in his shoulder revitalize instantly.

A woman suffering for several years with chronic pain and stiffness in the back of her neck was healed spontaneously during the third Attunement of The First Degree. She told the class that she saw a deep purple color, then white Light, felt enormous heat, then immense peace and a lifting away of the negative energy in her neck.

These examples reflect just a few of the many instances in which spontaneous healing or wholing has happened with The Radiance Technique. The universal, radiant energy accessed by TRT acts as a catalyst to trigger quantum leaps as described in new physics. In instantaneous healing a sudden transformation happens rather than a gradual change—a shift is made to direct contact with energy at a higher order. The old patterns and limits are transcended, and a new dimension is tapped.

15

The Gift of
The Radiance Technique®:
A New Beginning

> *Here is a test to find whether your mission on earth is finished: If you're alive, it isn't.*
> **Richard Bach**

A new stage of evolving Consciousness is happening for all of humanity, and simultaneously a "new age" is breaking for many of us from within ourselves. Advancing into the "new age" on a personal level means healing, wholing, growing, transforming, and going beyond or transcending your old limits, your old prejudices, your old angers, and your old escape mechanisms. It means taking a risk to find your own identity and maintaining a deep rather than a superficial sense of well-being, even when the waters get choppy and you seem to be tossed about on the rough waves of life. Through these transitions or passages in your own life, learning to identify with the ocean instead of the waves, so to speak, or, with the sky, instead of the passing clouds puts you in touch with what is Real and eternal within you. TRT accesses the gift of life, a natural energy-balancing and healing art and science that, in its essence, puts you in touch with your Real Self.

There is a wonderful Sufi story passed down for centuries which is entertaining, healing, wholing, and Enlightening! It goes like this:

> Once there was a powerful king, ruler of many lands, whose position was so great that wise men were his mere employees. Yet, one day, he felt himself confused so he summoned his sages. To them he said: "I do not know the cause, but something impels me to seek a certain ring. This ring will enable me to stabilize my confusion. I must have this ring and it must be one which will make me happy when I am unhappy, and at the same time, it must make me sad when I am happy and look upon it." The wise men consulted each other and threw themselves into deep reflection of the king's request. Finally, they arrived at a decision as to the nature of the ring which would satisfy their king.

> The ring which they designed had inscribed upon it the words:
> ## THIS, TOO, WILL PASS

The wholistic paradigm or model is designed to put you in touch with the whole—to include all that is in the cosmos and not to exclude even a particle. A "prescription for wholeness" begins with deciding at this point in your life the direction you want to go and includes being flexible and adaptable as your *process* unfolds in this life.

Tools for transformation are part of your journey. TRT is a powerful yet gentle, subtle science of connecting with life-force, Light energy of a higher order than you normally experience in daily life. TRT activating/attuning energy process is completely safe and harmless. It does not impose or impress energy on you but rather naturally aligns energy from within you. With use of TRT, you will be applying this natural life-force energy to your *whole* self, simultaneously balancing yourself physically, emotionally, mentally, and spiritually. With

TRT, you are directly accessing and amplifying your only true power—that which lies within you.

When used as instructed, TRT restores depleted vital energy and balances your energy naturally. Balancing energy on all levels of your being promotes healing, wholing, transformation, and, ultimately, Enlightenment. The Radiance Technique is a special gift—a unique method designed to put you in touch with and to amplify your inner strength and your inner truth.

One of the ways used by many people each day for activating the power within is by "affirmations"—the power of the spoken word. Affirmations combined with the Light-energy accessed by TRT give you an especially effective and quick way to quiet outer confusion, control scattered energies, connect *consciously* with your inner strength, and to promote ongoing mental clarity and stability.

One of the unique features of TRT is it can be used along with other techniques such as affirmations or even while doing other activities. An essential aspect of the gift of TRT is in its natural, universal quality. Doing some TRT hands-on head positions combined with saying affirmations such as, "I am whole, I am well, I am free," or "I know and I know that I know," centers you, heals you, wholes you, and Enlightens you.

Giving the gift of TRT to yourself gives Light-energy, vital energy to your body—a natural "food" for a natural organism! TRT is a direct way of having a positive effect on all levels of your Being, of promoting and maintaining positive wellness, and of expanding your awareness.

It has been said for centuries that *love* is the best healer and wholer. Love is a quality of the life-force, and TRT accesses Universal Love, Radiant energy. Love is not something you create. It is your True nature. For centuries, those who have been wise and awake have reminded us that we are Love and are Light in this world. TRT brings a gift of Light-energy that aligns you with your inner, natural integrity. Your hands are a gift through which you can direct this Cosmic Universal Love, Light-energy accessed by TRT. If for some reason you do not have use of your hands, TRT can be directed through other parts of your body or Being.

In the TRT Seminars, I often refer to TRT as accessing Radiant energy—a gift of the universe,—a gift of the cosmos. This

114

unique and ancient science of Light-energy has been preserved and passed intact through the centuries to be rediscovered as a Light-energy source now available to all of us as we step into a new age of humanity and a new age of ourselves. In one class, a woman experienced a deep and profound insight while meditating using TRT which she shared: "If everyone in the whole world took The Radiance Technique, we would have no more murders—no more wars." In her words, she captured the ultimate gift often discovered in using TRT—the gift of Life and the gift of honoring the Universal Light, within all of us.

I invite you to consider learning TRT, to give yourself the gift of TRT, to experience using this Cosmic Energy Science for yourself, and to incorporate it into your lifestyle in whatever ways are appropriate and special for you. Whatever your age, if you are alive you can learn, grow, and transform! One of the most profound aspects of the gift of TRT is in its putting you directly in touch with life-force, Radiant energy and freeing you into the awareness that every day is truly a *new beginning.*

16

Special Sharings from Students of The Radiance Technique®

When the book was originally written, most of the sharings were from people who had studied The First and The Second Degrees. In the years since then, more advanced students have studied The Third, The Fourth, The Fifth, The Sixth and The Seventh Degrees using The Radiance Technique® for some years. Some of their sharings are being made available to you in this Expanded Edition. What makes this a really special section is that the following sharings are unedited and have been written by the person involved in the interaction with The Radiance Technique®.

Miss Lola Hayes
The Fifth Degree
Master Vocal Teacher
Honorary Master/Teacher of The Radiance Technique®

(Miss Lola Hayes took The Fifth Degree when she was 81 years old. She is a Master vocal teacher and has been working with voice students for over forty years.)

For a very long time I, like countless others, had been moving on a journey toward Light and the Realization of my own True identity. Then in November of 1983, a clear vibrant Light shone brilliantly on my pathway in the person of Dr. Barbara Ray, who introduced me to The Real Reiki®, now also known as The Radiance Technique®, and started me spiralling counterclockwise up the pathway, while she held aloft her Beacon Light and lovingly beckoned to me to follow. How joyful and grateful I am that she with this remarkable technique came into my experience at that time and that I, for once in my life, didn't stop to rationalize but clasped her extended hand and ran as fast as I could behind her.

Now began my "Awakening Journey" and what an illuminative one it has been! During the Attunements of my First Degree, I was awake to another level of consciousness which I had contacted for brief fleeting moments before in my life. Later that evening, I realized that as I advanced I would have a tool with which I could penetrate and expand that consciousness. I have since then learned that I can bring that inner Light energy out into my present outer plane activity. As I was honored with Dr. Ray with The Second, The Third, The Fourth and now even The Fifth Degree, I have learned more and more assuredly how to access and expand this Radiant consciousness, "The Light within, with a living dynamic for everyday use."

I have integrated my expanded use of The Radiance Technique® with my life's work: guiding singers of all ages in the development of their vocal gifts. The singer, acquiring a workable technique, is also on an "Awakening Journey," searching for that which is already there waiting to be discovered: an *in place* process. I believe

116

that the artistic singer's complete and often hushed rapport with his or her audience is on the "Inner Plane."

Shanti to my Radiance family for their real, genuine, unconditional Love, and support. You have to experience it to believe it in this everyday world we seem to live in. Deep, deep, deep Shanti's to Dr. Barbara Ray–a guide of such extraordinary clarity, a True Master, with all-embracing capacity to love unconditionally all of God's creatures and creation. She so generously shares with all who will listen her profound awakeness and knowingness of Real Light, not the reflections, and gives us full direction for use of this special tool, The Radiance Technique®. I treasure the privilege of knowing her and studying with her. She is constantly opening gates and introducing me, unfolding gently, to the Inner World of my True Beingness. This is my Awakening Journey, ever ongoing.

Lola Hayes
The Seventh Degree

Miss Hayes continues to study and use The Seventh Degree in her 85th year.

On an unforgettable, clear, sparkling day in the summer of 1989, at the very top peak of a high mountain (Weisshorn, Switzerland)–surrounded and supported by my loving radiance family–I enjoyed the most humbling, at the same time elevating, experience of my life. That day, Dr. Barbara Ray, in her inner wisdom, boundless love and spiritual Light, gave me the special Attunement of The Seventh (and highest) Degree of The Radiance Technique.

From Dr. Ray's book, *The Expanded Reference Manual,* I quote: "The term Attunement and Attunement Processes have been used to describe the specific parts of this science which actually activate the radiance within and align you to your inner wholeness, giving you direct access to inner, universal, transcendental energy."

What an expansion! What a gift! What a responsibility!

Thus from this point of wholeness, I have expanded and been able to communicate more deeply with my singers to improve their singing as well as their contact and relationship with other human beings.

Alice Baily in *Serving Humanity* (page 428) tells us that "every expansion of consciousness resulting in an *increased scope of service* is to be taken at a cost and for this you will have to be prepared."

We shall have and continue to have tests from The First through The Seventh Degrees and beyond; but with this remarkable "tool," we can meet and pass them.

Believe me, I can testify.

Again, deep, deep, deep shantis and a heart filled with deep gratitude to Dr. Barbara Ray who so generously has shared this technique and its uses, which now are available to us.

And so my Awakening Journey continues into forever.

Barbara Aurora
The Fifth Degree
Teacher/Singer

As a performing artist and a teacher of singing, I have had the authentic experience of the profound benefits which The Radiance Technique® has brought to my capacities as an artist and as a teacher on all levels.

Through the use of hands-on applications and the use of Universal symbols and their processes, I have experienced a rich and luxuriant shift in sheen within the voice, not only its richness of quality but extension of range, ease and flexibility in projection of sound.

What I have experienced for myself has also been true of those whom I teach. Using principles of energy discovered through The Radiance Technique® and the process of Attunements with my clients, they have also experienced unfolding toward a whole radiant sound.

The Radiance Technique® assists in releasing stress. Once stress is released, the singer is free to use his "natural" instrument and the technique assists in his unfolding process to emit, generate, and radiate Light energy through the Throat Center with an expanded capacity for support with the body.

As I began to use The Radiance Technique® in my daily life, another wonderful process began to unfold. I found that what had once been stressful and agonizing situations for me began to be more objectively and subjectively observable. I began to feel serenity and continuity, seeing things from a greater perspective and expressing myself with greater clarity.

My awareness of myself, my emotions and thoughts and outer body, became clearly more perceptible as a means of knowing how I was relating with others and with myself. I began to view things as they really are!

I am experiencing a deep inner knowing of great love and compassion for the whole of humanity and all things manifest on this wonderful planet. Life is becoming a dance and not simply the unremitting episodes from one situation to the next. I am coming to know the *greater* sources of who I truly am.

A new spiritual dimension has opened for me, and I am understanding more fully the energy principles that are my "real" nature. The Radiance Technique® promotes from within the qualities of loving, wholeness, integrity, and self-realization. It is a harmonious resonance on all levels of our being. What more could I offer my students . . . what more could I offer myself? Yes, life *Is* a Celebration!

I am eternally grateful to Dr. Barbara Ray for preserving this magnificent and unique science of Universal energy.

Barbara Aurora
The Sixth Degree
Teacher/Singer

Through the natural expansion of The Fifth and The Sixth Degrees, new aspects support the unfolding process of life. Though there are times my life is very turbulent on one level, the steady compassionate energy of TRT has been the inherent essence supporting my life process.

While wishing that TRT would resolve my problems, which is *not* its purpose, I experienced a deepening capacity for Clarity, enabling me to observe my own issues. I have experienced shame and anger, simultaneously experiencing serenity. I have a choice to identify with these aspects, and in using TRT I am able to support and begin to heal the dead past.

What a joy to know my Radiant Touch is always in the NOW, emitting from within a principle of renewal and creativity.

In this past year as I unfold with The Fifth and The Sixth Degrees, within me there is a deeper awareness of the inner Radiant Heart as a real living essence resonating with the whole of my life. Awareness of my actions on every level is becoming clearer, and my choices toward harmlessness is becoming a choice of opportunity.

Through the use of the expanded Attunement Process, my healing and wholing have moved in ways I would have never thought possible. There is a deep peace and inner silence: the mind without thoughts within a dynamic of "Just Being."

I gave great gratitude to Dr. Barbara Ray for her commitment in protecting the integrity of this intact system and her great wisdom as a teacher and her unconditional love in bringing TRT forward for humanity.

Shannon Orrock
The Third Degree for Personal Growth (3A)
Entertainer, Comedienne

As an entertainer, I have many opportunities to use all three levels which I've studied so far. For every audience, I incorporate The Second and The Third Degree levels. While performing, I place one hand on my heart or throat from time to time—especially when I want to get a special point across.

By using the techniques learned at The Second and The Third Degrees, I can direct energy to the entire audience, to the room, to me and the audience, and to the whole situation.

I can direct Attunements through my Throat Center as I speak and sing. The latter is very important to me—to bring harmlessness to what I say, as much of comedy is anger turned sideways and has the potential to be harmful.

Reprinted with permission from The Radiance Technique® On The Job, Fred W. Wright Jr., published by Radiance Associates, © 1987.

Marvelle Lightfields
The Fifth Degree
Counselor/Writer/Lecturer

I want most to share how the application of "hands-on" has expanded for me through my own daily process with The Radiance Technique®. When I first took the technique in 1979, I had a very limited knowledge and relationship to the energy system that I actually am. Although I had practiced other techniques such as several disciplines of Yoga, they had given me what I came to consider as excellent introductory information on the Chakras or Centers of our human Life dynamic. Nothing had educated me the way my own Radiant hands have since that moment when I took The First Degree of The Radiance Technique®! My experiences have expanded with my applications of the whole session or with my own daily use of "hands-on" *all* the time! I counsel with people, and I use my hands on my own energy system throughout our sessions, replenishing *me* as I work with different energy levels to support them!

Each Degree of this technique had been a deepening of my awareness as my own capacity of expanding this Radiant energy has increased. I have had the joy of knowing and experiencing the differences in energy capacity within me as I have taken The Second Degree, The Third Degree, The Fourth Degree and The Fifth Degree. What a journey to knowingness of myself as an energy Being–as a vibrational and universal Being!

I know something from my own Chakras that no book can describe for me. When I am applying Radiant energy, I am inner aware of a sense of well-being and relaxation that is so centered and so whole as to be beyond anything else I have ever experienced. When I begin the patterns of the Cosmic Symbols–gateways to energy beyond form–in union with my hands-on, I am deepening a process where layers of accumulation of energy are being lightened and moved, being diffused with a soft and radiant lovingness that is beyond my emotional or mental planes to translate. What a shining Reality! I have a *real* experience of a different vibration than that which was there just moments before. And I know I am in resonance with a vibration of collective Wholeness that has existed always.

I have begun a journey with my Radiant hands, with my inner-connection with Cosmic Symbols and with the Attunement Processes where I can move into the awareness of the Eternal Consciousness. These moments occur and deepen within me as I am using The Radiance Technique®. They are gateways of Light inviting my exploration into more than moments.

I recently experienced a vibrant and meaningful awakening to the Real impact of the Throat Center (Chakra). I have used The Radiance Technique® to explore the outer voice and its manifestations in the outer world, and I have expanded my knowingness of the harm or harmlessness that comes through sharing words with one another through our voices in communication. Using the Attunement Process and The Fourth Degree, I have explored more of the opening Heart Center through speaking with awareness of harmlessness. I realize that the abuse of words–which are actually energy–can go unseen when the awareness of the Heart Center is not present. While meditating and attuning (with The Fifth Degree) with the Throat Center, I became aware that words on the page, such as letters written in anger or the haste of resentment, carry the full force and abuse of the Throat Center with them–to the page and to the person interacting with that page of paper and those seemingly harmless "words"! What a powerful energy of the Throat Center are words brought to paper for sharing with others. I continued my attuning and meditating and made a journey to the inner dimensions of myself to explore an even deeper discovery. All the wisdom of the Real Light has at varying times been brought into "print." I was particularly meditating with the great library of papyrus at Alexandria in Egypt. What a union of the great wisdom, put into manifestation for students of Eternal Truths that must have been. Now it is gone in its outer form, but the inner wisdom and energy principles have found their way into books of every truly great and Wise One who has come through the centuries after that time. I became aware of the deep and profound use of the Throat Center in carrying these "words" through the ages,

119

through the differing forms of language and yet always with the vibration of Light within them. These ways of expressing are not "words" from a mental plane, or they would never transcend and stand eternal through time. They are expressions in wholeness from the great and eternal consciousness through many "voices" that have been clear and have loved us enough to bring to us the energy behind the words of Truth—energy is forever.

This heightened realization in my meditation and Attunement Process has another inner-connected aspect. I am in an ongoing process of discovery with *The Expanded Reference Manual, The Official Handbook of The Radiance Technique®* and *The 'Reiki' Factor in The Radiance Technique®* as guides for my own growth in writing and speaking more clearly and as guides for my advanced study of The Radiance Technique®. My gratitude to Dr. Barbara Ray, my teacher, has expanded with this new awareness as I read each page knowing now how wholely she has once again brought more of these Eternal Truths and the Real energy of Love to me and to all of us in our search for inner wisdom and in our transforming process.

Marvelle Lightfields
The Sixth Degree
Counselor/Writer

In my ongoing process of becoming more aware of the expanded capacity that The Fifth and The Sixth Degrees have opened for me, I am realizing, with a piercing quality of "seeing", that my mental, emotional patterns are all self-evoked. They actually come from nowhere outside me, although they are totally supported by my culture, my professional encounters, and the world around me. This clarity comes in moments when I am least open to it, when I am deeply embedded in the superficial of my life. However, because I have the Light habit of hands-on, I use TRT for my own life every day. Somewhere in the beauty of my Radiant session, the mist clears and I can "see" again.

This simple realization has been written about by many people. All good psychology dotes on such revelations; all ordinary encounters espouse these kinds of awarenesses. However, the piercing Truth is that we can be self-actualized only as we live the wholeness of ourselves, not the superficial parts that are caught in patterns set long ago in our behavior.

Seeing the connections is only part of the picture; realizing the interconnection of all of these levels of energy at work simultaneously is truly awe-inspiring and gives me a humbling sense of wonder at how Radiant we all could be, that I can be. It is the fiber of my being, not the outer dress. However, the outer dressing had become such an over-emphasized part of my life to the point where my Real Self and my chance for realization of my true spiritual nature had receded to the recesses beyond daily awareness. Each day this piercing quality of Light-energy is more present in my awareness and I have Conscious choices to make. As I use TRT, in my hands-on session, or participating with the Cosmic Symbols or Attunement Processes, I move into seeing my wholeness in the Here Now. This awareness is the movement toward Consciousness that all the Great Ones have written about in order to guide us.

These great Truths that Dr. Barbara Ray has shared in this book and the others she has published have helped me to realize that the totally superficial life is filled with stress and striving. My service as a stress counselor has deepened as I become more Conscious that the relationship of the stressful outer self and its habits can block the deeper journey of the Real Self, which is a natural unfoldment into Enlightenment.

I have the joyful realization that TRT supports and sustains my Real Self to unfold into Consciousness and to keep expanding with the Eternal movement that is natural change and transformation.

Hilda Harris
The Fourth Degree
Opera Singer

(Hilda Harris is a world-renowned mezzo-soprano about whom "Essence Magazine" has written: "No list of the world's talented and attractive black divas would be complete without the name Hilda Harris.")

I use The Radiance Technique® a lot in my singing. I use the hands-on for myself for stress reduction, memory, for studying scores. And, the stress has diminished considerably.

Before studying The Radiance Technique®, if someone asked me to learn a new score, in say two weeks, I would say, "No." For a substantial role, it required not only learning music, but the lyrics as well, most of the time in a foreign language, plus research into the background of the character.

Now, using The Radiance Technique® speeds up the absorption process. Last year, I had two weeks to learn a major role of a world premiere opera. I'd sit with my hands in Head Position No. 2 and just go over the score and memorize.

And before I start the first rehearsal, I direct energy to the rehearsal and to everyone involved with the rehearsal, using my Third Degree techniques. Also, if anyone in the rehearsal is having problems, I use my Second and Third Degree techniques.

I have observed a steady improvement in my stamina since studying The Radiance Technique® in 1982. I don't get as nervous before a performance. There's so much support in the system. I can see the whole aura of the performance as well as the rehearsals–there seems to be a harmony that permeates the rehearsals and performances. I look in on other rehearsals going on at the same time elsewhere in the same opera house–you can feel a difference in the energy. During my voice lessons, I use Head Position No. 4 on my throat area and Front Position No. 1 over my heart. It's a way of communicating a feeling to the audience that I'm really bringing them into my heart and love is pouring out to them.

I also find that my voice is changing. It's in a process of change. My colleagues say they hear a different quality in my voice.

I know within myself there's another quality that's come in this year–more range and a depth of communication.

There's more of a fullness and this fullness not only is in the sound and in a different vibration. People say my voice, my sound touches them in a way they haven't been touched before. It's just spiraling. It really is spiraling.

Reprinting with permission from The Radiance Technique® Journal. January-March, © *1987.*

Dean M. Karns
The Third Degree for Personal Growth (3A)
Associate Professor, Music and Mathematics
    Chairman, Music Department

Since studying The Radiance Technique®, I rarely have a cold or a headache, and my sinuses are considerably cleared. I am only occasionally tired in the afternoons, and sleep well at night, usually six hours instead of the former eight.

I have found myself "working from a point of wholeness" in resolving difficult situations. Also, during the academic year, I attend several concerts and recitals. Each performance is, of course, an ideal time to do Attunements and use my Second Degree techniques for directing energy. Since sound is a vibration and permeates everything in a concert hall, sound is an ideal medium to carry an Attunement. So now when listening to a performance, I Attune the sound with the intent that performers and audience alike will benefit from the expanded energy.

Reprinted with permission from The Radiance Technique® On The Job, Fred W. Wright Jr., published by Radiance Associates, © *1987.*

Radiant Networking For World Peace

Katherine Lenel
The Fourth Degree
Radiant Vocal Expansion[sm]

Each issue of this column supports a daily High Noon networking for world peace. All alumni of The Radiance Technique® are encouraged to participate for from five to thirty minutes (or more) at 12 noon each day in their time zone. Networking is co-creative! You can use your radiant hands on your heart and image the planet. You can use a globe or a picture of the earth to correspond for the planet. Those who know some of the Cosmic Symbols on which The Radiance Technique® is based can use them to direct energy, and those who are able to use the Attunement Process can attune the planet. We can align all of our energies to the level of peace and harmony which is the source of our life. Remember: When we join together to generate light, the energy squares by the number of those participating.

This quarter we are focusing on radiant babies. It is easy to see the source of vitality and love shining out of babies' eyes and mirrored in their unfailing spontaneity. We can build a safe place for that love to grow whenever we use The Radiance Technique®.

The joy and wonder that is the birthright of all children can be reclaimed by people of any age and awakened in all living creatures through the use of the profound tool we have studied. Imagine a world in which the energy and aliveness of children matured into a glowing compassion and creativity that did not decrease with age. Imagine a world where plants, animals, and human beings just naturally co-operate in nurturing and expanding life for the good of all. Such is the nature of universal energy, the source of life, and such are the gifts of using the tool for tapping that source—The Radiance Technique®.

At noon each day in your time zone, support the rise of awareness and love on the earth by using your radiant hands and heart to network for Peace on Earth.

Reprinted with permission from The Radiance Technique® Journal, *Winter, © 1988.*

Wesley Balk, Ph.D.
The Fifth Degree
Professor/Teacher, Acting, Singing, Performing; Author

Attunements before, during, and after the teaching process are my principal tools. Hands-on—especially in these sense of touch—is quite often possible when working with performers.

Since studying The Radiance Technique®, my overall vitality has markedly increased. I have received dozens of comments from people who have worked with me as to the remarkable changes in my teaching.

Also, opportunities have "flowed" in a different way, with unexpected offers. In my writing and teaching, there is a much stronger sense of purpose and coherence. In my writing, ideas flow with markedly different freedom—there is more openness, more connectedness, more wholeness in my approach.

Reprinted with permission from The Radiance Technique® On The Job, *Fred W. Wright Jr., published by Radiance Associates, © 1987.*

Demeter Sierra
The Fifth Degree
Opera Singer

As a singer of opera and concerts, I have found a profound change since studying The Radiance Technique®. It may seem to be outer changes—for indeed my voice has changed—but it is an inner science and originates deep within and spirals into outer manifestations. I use hands-on during study periods—the second and third head positions in particular. The Radiance Technique® facilitates memorization. Then I also use my hands-on during rehearsals and often the hands over the adrenals. It does not attract attention and energizes and helps balance my performing. Also keeping the Cosmic Symbols going, moving as I am moving through the music, has changed an aspect of my singing I would never have dreamed possible. I am free to improvise. This had always been a great problem for me—to have the confidence to allow music to pour from me, wordless sounds at times which come from deep inside a source in me. People who have known my work over the years have commented on a freer, richer, and more expansive sound—and it is constantly expanding.

I am deeply grateful to be living in a time when the marvelous art and science has been made available to us through Dr. Barbara Ray. In deeper studies, I have come to a deeper knowing of myself and the expansion into exciting unknown territory! We truly can be all we are meant to be—and working with The Radiance Technique® has far-reaching effects.

As well as being a singer and teacher, I have also worked extensively with animals from pets to injured seal mammals and even while milking cows! Once touch is established, animals will most often relax and trust. The vibration is unspoken communication with them, and the more one uses The Radiance Technique®, the more the vibration expands.

I have much, much gratitude and joy for having this technique and the capacity to grow and expand with every living breath.

Clarity James
The Fourth Degree
Singer/Vocal Teacher

My diagnosis of cancer of the cervix came at a time last year when my performing schedule was quite full. I received the information on a Friday and was due the following Monday to begin rehearsing for a concert with a major symphony orchestra on the West Coast, to be followed immediately by a summer festival Wagner Ring Cycle. The moment I received the diagnosis, I networked for energy. That I had always received tremendous physical support from using The Radiance Technique® (reduction of pain, facilitation of the healing process) was a given. What I was to become more profoundly aware of on this journey was the depth of support for my emotional, mental, and spiritual bodies as well.

The protocol for my treatment was internal, then external radiation. During that process, I was continually amazed that I could actually keep a clear head and look at all my choices and persist in asking for what I felt would be most supportive for all concerned. Oh yes, there was the "why me—poor me—woe is me" syndrome, AND I never stayed there long, so great was the nurturing and support of The Radiance Technique®. I experienced in a very tangible way the cradling net of loving energy that was directed towards me from all over the planet, as well as luxuriating in a great many hands-on sessions with what I called my resident "band of angels." No matter what else was going on physically, emotionally, or mentally, I always had an awareness of that great Cosmic Hug that was there for me—all I had to do was to choose to consciously walk into it and allow it to support me.

One of the most exciting discoveries of my use of this technique was during the actual implant process. I had insisted upon using a local anesthetic so that there could be no possible damage to my larynx from tubes going through my throat as could have been the case with a general anesthetic. This request naturally met with some resistance from both surgeon and anesthesiologist; however, I persisted and they finally agreed. Although the implant was quite uncomfortable physically, I experienced existing in total wholeness on other levels of my Being! I became the dance of our Energy Model! I observed myself and the physical process in a simultaneity of different levels of energy. At the same time that I was, indeed, intensely involved in the physical, I also KNEW that my SELF was much more than that. I did not discount the physical, nor try to escape from it AND there was more. Using all the levels of The Radiance Technique® that were available to me, I touched into that place of wholeness within me and experienced resting there in total safety, no matter what was going on on the outer. The implant went very smoothly and quickly—I left the hospital a day early and flew two days later to my next job.

Throughout the six weeks of rehearsals and performances of the Wagner, I continued to experience expanded support from my use of The Radiance Technique® and was able to perform well on all levels, no one having the slightest notion that I was not totally well.

Back home in New York, as I began the five weeks of daily radiation treatments, I realized that this was to be the time that I was most grateful for The Radiance Technique®. I would set up a directing process during the treatment, imaging protecting the healthy cells while simultaneously allowing the cancerous cells to "go up" in light, as well as wrapping our Cosmic Symbols protectively around different areas of my physical body that might be feeling particularly vulnerable on any given day. I also directed energy towards other people going through similar processes, and even towards the machine itself, imaging the radiation from the machine traveling through the symbols as it entered my body.

Riding the subway daily to my treatment also presented a great many opportunities to get beyond myself and offer this energy to others. That also proved to be the case in the waiting area of the treatment center. Often, instead of anxiety or fear, I would experience a great fullness in my heart, as I would feel beckoned by a fellow patient to share this energy on the inner planes.

My non-stop use of hands-on throughout this process not only made the physical discomfort much less uncomfortable but also gave me a noticeable vitality uncommon to people who go through such treatments. Upon attending my first group therapy session, some of the staff assumed that I was there as friend or relative, not as a patient. The therapist saw that I was somehow different from her other clients. She said she saw in me the ability to go out of and beyond the physical and psychological pain and questioned me about that process. After discussing The Radiance Technique® with her, she decided to take the seminar and now uses this energy on herself and others.

My WHOLE (pun intended) attitude on this journey has probably surprised me more than anyone. When I first heard the words "malignant," I began looking at my life quite differently. I became more willing to be much more involved in the Here Now awareness that exists at the center of The Radiance Technique®. I continue to learn that no matter what part of my being is in distress, The Radiance Technique® gives me the ability to wholistically and naturally support whatever process I'm going through. I experience new depths of Trust and Love and Gratitude that we've been given such a tool here now on Planet Earth.

Yesnie Carrington
The Fifth Degree
Business/Stress Management

This sharing is from my experience when I had the opportunity to spend a week in West Berlin. I was most fortunate to visit, almost daily, the world-famous zoo which is located in the heart of downtown. The zoo's setting is in a large green area, complete with much water, flowers, and trees, and the designers have laid out the animals' homes in such a fashion that you can walk very close to them.

I was impressed with the number of species of animals, as well as the variety within the different species. For example, the zoo had five different kinds of bears from all over the world, in addition to a Giant Panda from China. The variety of deer was beyond my attempt to count.

I had the incredible opportunity to exchange some hands-on application of universal energy as well as Attunements with Nikki, a three-month-old tiger cub! With each Attunement, Nikki became more and more relaxed—de-stressing from the rigors of zoo living! It was my first chance to share this universal energy with a non-domesticated animal. And there was an instant knowingness from Nikki of the universal vibration.

With each species, I was directly able to contact their universal, inner planes and know consciously of our interconnection by using the directing of energy and the Attunement Processes. And I could observe their awareness of the symbols and Attunements instantly. I had a direct knowingness also of their intelligence and of this recognition of universal energy by them, and sometimes their outer form would express this knowingness, this recognition.

A personal experience with a hippopotamus is a good example of this. There were four adult hippos in the zoo living in a rather contained water area. Each day one particular hippo responded most obviously to me when I began using the Cosmic Symbols and Attunements.

On my last day at the zoo, the hippo began wildly splashing water with its head, in all directions, while the other three remained calm and generally in a resting position of being almost fully under water.

The lions always roared loudly with the symbols and Attunements. The deer sat very quiet and still as if they were listening to the universal vibration. The two-hump camels actually walked toward me.

With this science of universal energy, I had my own direct knowingness of the inner planes of each of these wonderful species, and I knew that I was directly contributing to their wellness and wholeness. I encourage others to share The Radiance Technique® with animals in this way. I know that I had a communion with these animals unlike any before!

Reprinted with permission from The Radiance Technique® Journal, *October-December,* © *1986.*

Fred W. Wright Jr.
The Fourth Degree
Writer

Before taking The First Degree of The Radiance Technique® in June 1981, there were many times in my life when I felt helpless or powerless. Whenever someone close to me became ill, or whenever I found myself faced with a challenge that didn't offer an immediate solution, I felt helpless. I felt as if events were out of my control.

In the face of world crises—war, famine, major disasters—I felt especially powerless. My mind easily and quickly said to me: "What can I do about the threat of nuclear war? I'm only one person. I'm not a politician or a powerful world figure. There's nothing I can do. What can I do about famine in Africa? I'm not rich enough or powerful enough to make a difference. There's nothing I can do."

As I began to use the methods learned at the various degrees of The Radiance Technique®, I began to realize a sense of something growing and expanding in my awareness—and it was a sense of power, of the power of radiant energy. As I networked with my technique for people and events throughout the world, I began to feel within me a surge of *confidence* and *community*.

And as I began to feel less alone and less apart from the rest of the world, I began to feel less helpless, and more able to make a difference.

The Radiance Technique® has thus been a consistently changing and expanding experience for me. I feel part of a vast network of energy that is balancing, supporting and, yes, powerful in a whole, unconditional way. I feel much more a part of events in the world, and much more responsible for what I can do to help this planet, and all five billion of us on it, to be more unified and more loving with one another.

"Radiant Power" is no longer just an idea with me; it is an energy that I am experiencing each and every day with an unknown number of other beings on the plant.

Joseph Gifford
The Fourth Degree
Professor Emeritus, Performing Arts

I use The Radiance Technique® in my work in all kinds of ways. Frequently, I would give an Attunement to the class as a whole at the beginning or end of the class. This helped them to help themselves in using their time and energy more constructively. Students came to me with physical problems—headaches, injuries—which I would use hands-on positions with, or if there wasn't time, then by directing this energy to them in the evening.

I used The Second and The Third Degree techniques constantly to lessen tension in myself and my students and colleagues, to bring about more inner and outer peace, to create a more harmonious, unifying, caring and sharing environment.

As a teacher, I find The Radiance Technique® helps me be more efficient and more creative. I find I am communicating with grater clarity, greater depth of understanding of my students and the material I am teaching. By attuning myself at least 15 to 25 times a day, I find my intuitional powers have increased greatly. I am less concerned with matters of duality. I see more clearly.

Reprinted with permission from The Radiance Technique® On The Job, *Fred W. Wright Jr., published by Radiance Associates,* © *1987.*

Marilyn Alvey
The Fifth Degree
Legal Secretary

In early November I met a beautiful little Siamese kitten that I wanted to bring into my home and having an older cat, I began daily to do Attunements and to direct radiant energy to each of them for about five days before bringing her home.

A network of people also were directing energy on a daily basis to them. I did hands-on with Flower Face (the older cat) and told her how great it would be for her to have another kitty friend to play with and to love, and to keep her company when I was away.

Starlight came home with me in a kitty carrier. Flower Face circled the cage and growled, peering inside at the cowering little one. Speaking gently to both of them, I again attuned and directed energy to them. Flower Face stopped growling and began rubbing against me. I held her in my lap, doing hands-on and assuring her that I loved her dearly and that Starlight had come to be with both of us.

Starlight spent the night in the bathroom as a protective measure, and Flower Face cuddled closely that night as I continued attuning the relationship between them. At 3 a.m., Starlight woke me mewing quite loudly. I went into the bathroom, sat on the floor and held her in my Heart Center, doing hands-on for a long time, and she went back to sleep till morning.

When we awoke, I let Starlight out to explore the house, and after a while, I opened the door and Flower Face growled and hissed while Starlight jumped around her and cowered at the growling.

I watched and continued to direct radiant energy as they interacted together. I kept the new kitten in the bathroom that day while I was working and kept attuning and directing energy. When I got home, they both mewed and purred, welcoming me home.

I let Starlight out, and after a few minutes of Flower Face growling, sniffing, making a few swats at the new Siamese kitten and getting acquainted, off they ran together, chasing through the house. In an ordinary sense, this was an amazing event—just 24 hours after I brought the new kitten home, they were romping and playing together.

What a joy to direct the unconditional, loving energy of The Radiance Technique® and to watch the cats as they experience and express that energy in their lives. They are very loving cats, to me and to each other. They sometimes sit on my lap all wrapped around each other, purring their love and contentment.

They are now the best of friends, playing, jostling, chasing one another, sleeping together and wrapped up together, and often they do paws-on with each other. Yes, of course, they both have been attuned to The Radiance Technique®. Celebration!"

Reprinted with permission from The Radiance Technique® and The Animal Kingdom, by Marvelle Lightfields, published by Radiance Associates © 1992.

Leslie Christopher
The Fourth Degree
Registered Nurse

When I was completing my nursing training as a student at Johns Hopkins University, TRT supported me in so many ways. And I can't imagine my nursing practice without it.

The Radiance Technique enhances all the other nursing skills I have learned. When I take a temperature, I can share an Attunement with the patient at the same time. When I change wound dressings, I pattern Cosmic Symbols into the wounds. When I give a patient a bath, I am conscious of the Radiant Touch of my hands.

In the operating room, I've been able to hold a patient's hand while he or she is going under general anesthesia and do Attunements during the operation with the surgical staff as well as the patient.

One patient told me of a past suicide attempt, and I sat and listened with one hand on my Heart Center and did Attunements on the inner planes the whole time he

126

talked. Another of my patients was on a ventilator and unconscious, and as I cared for her I did hands-on her Heart Center and I also did Attunements for her. No matter what the condition my patients are in, with TRT I have a means of supporting them. Even in the face of a painful procedure, numerous machines or the dying process, I don't feel helpless, no matter what the situation.

With TRT, I am not limited to outer gestures, and I am not dependent solely on my personality. I can weave radiant support for the patient with Cosmic Symbols, Attunements and my Radiant Touch.

Reprinted with permission from The Radiance Technique® On The Job, by Fred W. Wright Jr., © 1992, Radiance Associates.

Crystal Sierra
The Fifth Degree
Animal Caretaker

In ongoing celebration of the Purposes of The Radiance Technique Association (TRTAI), I want to share how these purposes deeply inner-connect with a very special part of my life–volunteering at the California Marine Mammal Center.

The Center is an animal care facility for sick and injured lions and seals. It has as its purpose the 'rescue, rehabilitation and release" of these vital marine mammals. These animals are wild when rescued and great care is taken to support their wildness so that they can fully function upon their return.

Over the months I have helped at the Center, I have become increasingly aware of how *natural* and *understanding* the energy of these 'wild' creatures is. I interact with the essence of the wildness–that 'just being'–through the use of The Radiance Technique®, a cosmic, natural science, and find my awareness of the Natural harmony of the essence of all life is expanding, expanding, expanding!

In the continuum of rescue, rehabilitation and release, I use the precise system for accessing radiant energy through the use of hands-on application, the directing of energy through the Cosmic Symbols and the Attunement Process.

When a rescue call comes into the Center, I inner-connect the radiant energy with the image of the animal before we arrive on the scene–to help ease any stress the animal may be in–and especially in the transition from the beach to the animal's new temporary 'home' at the Center.

Once the animals are set up in their own large pens (complete with pool!), the volunteer crews are then responsible for their care/rehabilitation–from feeding to medicating to cleaning their pens. I will often 'clean' their pens with radiant energy, using the application of the Cosmic Symbols, as well as physically scrubbing them out.

Feeding times are always a special joy as I toss fish into the pools. And since I help prepare their meals, my radiant 'heart hands' touch a lot of fish! That way I share my radiant touch even if I cannot directly touch the seals and sea lions (they can and do bite humans).

For the sicker animals, we 'tub feed' them a fish mash formula. This "tub feeding" process can be quite a struggle for everyone involved, both humans and animals. If I am the person restraining the animal (holding him still), I gently place my hands on his head and direct energy with the Cosmic Symbols. I have experienced an energy of calmness moving through the animal for the duration of the feeding process.

When breaks occur in our duties, I often walk around to the pens and inner-act with each seal or sea lion. It is in these moments of oneness with these beings that I experience a quiet peace–and such gratitude for this profound science.

It is through these radiant communications that I can use The Second Degree technique of correspondence to inner-connect the animals to their species out in the ocean. I know I am supporting them *all* on the inner, even at this moment in time when their outer environment is increasingly becoming more polluted by oil spills, toxic chemicals, dumps, etc.

Some animals die during their stay, while others recover and are released. Both types of 'releases' are profound–and I have experienced the vibration of an animal that just died, using that opportunity to support and nurture its being during transition.

For those animals released into the Pacific, I will direct energy to them throughout the following months, supporting them in their natural habitat, and 'remembering' them in my heart.

Yes! Such are the precious opportunities to 'aid in service to all Life Forms' (one of the purposes of the TRTAI) through the marine mammals and the use of TRT. These animals have expanded and continue here-now to expand within me the knowingness of True Service and True Inner-Connection to and for Life in all its magnificent forms here on Earth.

Reprinted with permission from The Radiance Technique® *and The Animal Kingdom, by Marvelle Lightfields,* © *1992, Radiance Associates.*

Fred W. Wright Jr.
The Fourth Degree
Writer/Editor/Teacher

The joy of participating in this Expanded Edition leads me to a re-awakening to the wonderful empowering this book and The Radiance Technique bring to the world. First of all, I had the joy to be involved in the first-ever printing of the original manuscript in 1980. And in some of the years since then I have had the opportunity to assist as an editor in the preparation of the Expanded Edition. In the here now, I am in the midst of helping as an editor and proofreader with the new and even more expanded edition, and it has been a profoundly touching experience. As I read and reread these chapters, I am frequently filled with wonder at the profound wisdom that Dr. Barbara Ray has placed within these pages.

I cannot read these chapters and not continually ask myself why *everyone* who reads these pages doesn't immediately seek out the nearest Authorized Instructor and the closest seminar. The Radiance Technique can embrace and expand absolutely everything within this infinite universe to which it is applied. What incredible potential this book reveals!

This book speaks to me anew each time I spend time with it. That, to me, is the true measure of a book–that it transcends the few years, in the sense of centuries and civilizations, during which it is printed and sold. This book offers power to any individual in the world, regardless of nationality or language, who feels powerless in the face of events and forces that seem greater than a human can bear. This book reminds me that The Radiance Technique empowers me to realize I *can* make a difference with every single energy, dark or light, that comes into my life. (1992)

Marvelle Lightfields
The Sixth Degree
Counselor/Writer

I am serving as a helper in the editing and preparation of this book and in the process, many of these "working" moments have been deeply touching and rewarding, true moments of expansion of my Real Self. I am in this moment touched by this book in ways that go beyond what is written on the page in front of me. I, too, share a continuum of having helped with the original manuscript and in the celebratory realization of that, I am pierced by the beauty of this book. I am joyous that this particular volume will reach many thousands who may have never read the original book.

The beauty and inspiration come from the writer, Dr. Barbara Ray, who celebrates life and in the process brings to each reader the joy of possibility. Every chapter of this book uplifts the heart, renews the knowledge that each of us is more than just the outer parts–we have an inner spark of Light beyond our comprehension. Just reading and exploring the many sharings of love and tenderness, and of joy and renewal that are here has broadened my own life. For you see, TRT makes a difference first in your own life, and then expansively in the lives of all around you! That is the opportunity you have long been waiting for! (1992)

128

17

Radiant Interactions

You are invited to deepen your awareness of the inner meanings of some of the wisdom and refections that are put here for your radiant interaction. Students who have studied TRT will be using the techniques they have learned in their seminars to support them while they are reading. For students of TRT and others who have not yet studied the technique, it is important to set aside a meditative or quiet time and choose to read some or all the following quotes. As you read, use these quotations to become more involved in your own inner process of growth and transformation, and let yourself remain the observer of what happens. It is suggested that you explore and discover with new eyes what responses you have at different times of meditation and reflection, supporting yourself to go beyond the level of the mind to seek the real vibration beyond the words on these pages.

Selections from Barbara Ray:

"Love is the only Purpose of Life.

Love is the only Reason for Living.

Love is the only Power.

LOVE is All there Is."

"We are citizens of the Radiant Inner Heart."

"Animals and plants are an integral part of our planetary system, and their destiny is linked with ours."

"Remember–Your Awakening is a Journey, not a destination."

"The joy of material things fades away but the Joy of the Soul never fades–the Soul is in Eternal Love with Spirit–its Joy is indescribable!"

"All the great world teachers and all the mystics, known and unknown, have taught the truth about your real nature that 'You are the Light of the World.' . . . Each of us has the opportunity through expanded Consciousness to *know* it for ourselves and to *act* as though we know it. When you *consciously* know that you are Light, you can *emit* only unconditional love, brotherhood, wholeness, radiance and the will-to-good toward your fellow Beings."

"Enlightenment is your Cosmic Birthright."

"The part is not greater than the Whole, cannot overcome the Whole and does not function as The Whole."

"The Law of Transformation is natural to us. We are transforming all the time."

"Consciousness is not more and more of Awareness."

"I am
You Are
We are
Unity in Diversity."

"It's not what you *think* you are doing.
It's not what you *say* you are doing.
It's not what you *feel* you are doing.
It's what you are *actually* doing."

"The Inner dynamic of this science (TRT) is a process of Wholes, not parts."

"You need nothing outside of Yourself to Wake Up."

"When you increase your capacity to receive, you also increase your capacity to give."

"Discovery is Here Now. It is *always* happening."

"All Awakened Ones reveal that the path to Enlightenment begins within the Heart—the Real Inner Heart. Discovering your Inner Forever Heart is 'The Awakening Journey®'of Universal Radiant Light."

"Discovering who you really are, getting in touch with your true self, expanding your sphere of consciousness, and *consciously* becoming one with your source is an incredibly sacred, beautiful journey toward wholeness."

Selections from others:

"Up to the Twentieth Century, reality was everything humans could touch, smell, see, and hear. Since the initial publication of the chart of the electromagnetic spectrum . . . humans have learned that what they can touch, smell, see, and hear is less than one-millionth of reality."
    Albert Einstein

"Sometimes our light goes out but is blown again into flame by an encounter with another human being. Each of us owes the deepest thanks to those who have rekindled this inner light."
    Albert Schweitzer

"One can never consent to creep when one feels the impulse to soar."
    Helen Keller

"The more faithfully you listen to the voice within you, the better you hear what is sounding outside."
    Dag Hammarsjold,
    former Secretary General of the United Nations

"Harmony requires that each part should fulfill its particular function in relationship to the whole. . . ."
J.C. Cooper

"Experience is a mere peephole through which glimpses come down to us of eternal things."
George Santayana

"The most beautiful thing we can experience is the mysterious. It is the source of all true art and science."
Albert Einstein

"Man's capacity for consciousness alone makes him man."
Carl Jung

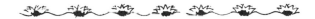

"If I don't know I don't know, I think I know."
R. D. Laing

"The drawing in of the universal energy by a conscious action of the higher powers of the being from around or from above, by a call to what is still to us a transcending consciousness . . . or descent from the transcendence itself, may well become an occasional, a frequent, or a constant phenomenon. . . ."
Sri Aurobindo

"The best and the most beautiful things in the world cannot be seen or even touched. They must be felt with the heart."
Helen Keller

"Real Knowledge, truth, is only gained through this direct experience; all else is merely knowledge 'about' something.
J.C. Cooper

"I did not arrive at my understanding of the fundamental laws of the universe through my rational mind."
Albert Einstein

"I am not a thing—a noun. I seem to be a verb, an evolutionary process—an integral function of the universe."
R. Buckminster Fuller

"The difference between transformation by accident and transformation by a system is like the difference between lightning and a lamp. Both give illumination, but one is dangerous and unreliable, while the other is relatively safe, directed, available."
Marilyn Ferguson

"Out yonder there lies a huge world which exists independently of human beings and which stands before us like a great eternal riddle . . . the contemplation of that riddle beckons like a liberation."
Albert Einstein

"Something can be a part only if there is a Whole to be a part of."
David Bohm
Unfolding Meaning

"We see the world piece by piece, as the sun, the moon, the animal, the trees. We live in succession, in division, in parts and particles. Meantime, within man is the soul of the whole, the wise silence, the universal beauty to which every part and particle is equally related, the Eternal One."
Ralph Waldo Emerson

"When we try to pick out something by itself, we find it hitched to everything else in the universe."
John Muir,
Founder, The Sierra Club

"We know who speaks for the nations. But who speaks for the human species?"
Carl Sagan

"Heart could reply directly to heart, the life-force come to the help of other lives and answer their call in spite of strangeness and distance. . . ."
Sri Aurobindo

"Life unfolds its wealth and beauty according to the unveilment or expansion of consciousness. . . . I soar in the plane of silence over the peaks of highest wisdom."
Paramahansa Yogananda

"Lead me from the Unreal to the Real,

From Darkness to Light,

From Death to Immortality."
    Upanishads

"All Truth passes through three stages. First, it is ridiculed. Second, it is violently opposed. Third, it is accepted as being Self-evident."
    Schopenhauer

"We shall require a substantially new manner of thinking if mankind is to survive."
    Albert Einstein

"Experience is not what happens to you; it's what you make of what happens to you."
    Aldous Huxley

"What lies behind you and what lies before you are tiny matters compared to what lies within you."
    Ralph Waldo Emerson

"To be confused about what is different and what is not, is to be confused about everything."
    David Bohm
    Wholeness and the Implicate Order

"Learn to listen to the voice of Love within you. Live Love; practice feeling it within and expressing it without."
　　　Paramahansa Yogananda

"Enlightenment is being awake in the nowness."
　　　Chogyam Trungpa

"From joy does spring all creation, by joy it is maintained, towards joy does it progress and into joy does it enter."
　　　Tagore

"Humans are as much a part of the fabric of the cosmos as a moon rock, an ice particle in the rings of Saturn, or an astcroid in a galaxy a billion light-years away. We are all star-stuff, assemblages of atoms cooked in the thermonuclear fires at the hearts of stars. . . ."
　　　Terence Dickinson
　　　The Universe and Beyond

"May the *Great Mystery* make sunrise in your heart."
　　　Sioux Indian

"We are all starfolk."
　　　Carl Sagan

"You are a spark of Eternal Flame. You can hide the spark, but you can never destroy it."
Paramahansa Yogananda

"For the rest of my life, I want to reflect on what light is . . ."
Albert Einstein, 1916

"The breeze at dawn has secrets to tell you.
Don't go back to sleep.

You must ask for what you really want.
Don't go back to sleep.

People are going back and forth
across the doorsill
where the two worlds touch.

The door is round and open.
Don't go back to sleep."
Rumi
Open Secret—Versions of Rumi

18

Selected Excerpts from
The Expanded Reference Manual of The Radiance Technique®

The following excerpts are only a few of the more than 600 entries in *The Expanded Reference Manual*, by Barbara Ray, Ph.D., which is a unique "A to Z" of ways to use TRT in your daily life. *The Expanded Reference Manual* is designed for students and alumni of every Degree of TRT and has references that offer guidance for using radiant energy to deepen your personal growth and development. It is also a book for people who have never studied TRT, for it is both valuable and beneficial to people in their personal growth and transformation on the Path of Awakening, even if they have not yet studied The Radiance Technique®. To learn this technique you will need to be taught by a fully qualified, currently certified Authorized Instructor. Furthermore, *The Expanded Reference Manual* is so comprehensive that serious students of Consciousness will be using it for centuries to come. (*The Expanded Reference Manual* is available to the public and additional information on this and other books is on the Addresses page.)

EXERCISE–Although The Radiance Technique® is *not* a substitute for exercise, it *is* an incredible support for using before, during and after your exercise program for restoring depleted energy, for balancing and wholing areas which need special support, for relaxing and releasing stored tensions and dense or negative patterns, and for expanding, enhancing and enlightening your entire process of wellness and wholeness, and for emotional and mental centering and calming and *stabilizing*. **SEE ALSO: AEROBICS, ATHLETES, CALMING, CAMPING, CENTERING, ENDURANCE, ENERGIZING, RUNNING, WALKING, YOGA, ZEST.**

HAPPINESS–In the ever-shifting cycles of the degrees of the polarity of "happy–unhappy", you can use TRT for gaining deeper insights into the nature of these cycles and for expanding your sense of happiness. Universal energy is not polarity or partial energy so it cannot make you feel happy or unhappy–rather it supports you in whatever aspect of these cycles you are in and can transform your consciousness to a higher state. **SEE ALSO: CHOICE, DUALITIES, EXPANDING, LOVING, POLARITY, UNIVERSAL.**

ANIMALS–One of the greatest joys is using TRT with animals and pets of all kinds. All animals respond each in their own way from within when contacted with this radiance. When possible the hands-on application usually allows for a special radiant energy bond between you and the pet. When the hands-on application is not possible or appropriate (such as with untamed or wild animals), you would need to learn the use of The Second Degree or beyond to access, activate and direct this radiant energy. On the living planet Earth there are many kingdoms all in an unfolding process. What a profound opportunity for supporting and "inner-connecting" with the animal kingdom in its journey to Light. We are *ALL*, in our True Inner Light, one essence. For a more extensive discussion, please see the book *The Radiance Technique® and The Animal Kingdom*, by Marvelle Lightfields, which has selections from hundreds of sharings on all aspects of using TRT with animals. Such subjects as adopting an animal, going through the death and dying process, interacting with animals who are injured and healthy, domestic and in the wild, are covered in the book. See information on the Addresses page. **SEE ALSO: BIRDS, CATS, DOGS, HORSES, NATURE, PLANTS, RELAXATION.**

140

CAMPING–TRT is a perfect energy science for camping, hiking, mountaineering and any other outdoor activity or sport. You can access the Universal energy within and expand upon it *any place, any time and without* the need for additional equipment or supplies. TRT goes where you go, naturally. TRT allows you the opportunity for expanding your profound experiences of the natural world, itself, and in relationship to you and all living life forms on Earth. As a Cosmic Universal energy science, this technique is also a "gateway" to the deeper awakenings of your "inner-connection" with Earth cycles, with the Solar System and with the Universe as a whole. **SEE ALSO: CLIMBING, COSMIC, ENERGIZING, EXERCISE, KARATE, NATURAL COSMIC SCIENCE, NATURE, SAILING, TAI CHI, UNIVERSAL.**

JOB, "ON-THE-JOB"–TRT is an excellent resource for use "on-the-job," allowing you the opportunity to restore and balance yourself on-the-spot with universal, wholing radiant energy–and with no special tools or devices needed! Using one hand or two you can be constantly supporting your activities in any work setting. Use of TRT on-the-job can deepen your creativity, help balance and energize you, support your relaxation and the reduction of the stresses of the work environment, and open you to the expansion of your capacities in the work you've chosen to do. In his compilation for the book *The Radiance Technique® On The Job, Expanded Edition*, Fred W. Wright Jr. has collected and shared how secretaries and opera singers, attorneys and plumbers, massage therapists and salespeople, counselors and contractors–hundreds of people in differing professions and work situations–are using this radiant support "on-the-job". See information on the Addresses page. **SEE ALSO: COSMIC SCIENCE, CREATIVITY, DENSE, ENERGIZING, ENERGY, PRODUCTIVITY, RELAXATION, STRESS, VOICE, WELLNESS, WHOLENESS.**

CANCER–TRT can be applied as a harmless support system accessing Radiance as your life journey unfolds in cycles with polarities of wellness and illness. TRT is *not* a technique or science of disease but is a science for accessing and *using* in your daily life, whole, Universal, Radiant energy which interacts in a benevolent way with lower non-universal energies whether they are positive or negative. TRT is also helpful when chemotherapy or radiation treatments are needed. TRT is profound in supporting your journey to wholeness on *all* planes of your Being. Health is one aspect of your life process and is not the *whole* of your Being. TRT is a cosmic energy science which can give you entrance into your inner planes while helping you to become aware of the nature of your outer planes and their *relationship* to the whole. TRT can also help you with stress and with expanding your *quality of life* in whatever aspect of your process you are experiencing. **SEE ALSO: A.I.D.S., CALMING, MEDITATION, RELAXATION, STRESS, WHOLENESS.**

DISCOVERY PROCESS—In higher consciousness growth this refers to the process of being able to move into the unknown without pre-evaluating the experience, without trying to limit by comparisons and analysis. Discovery is going beyond the known limits or boundaries. Discovery is a natural inner energy which nature has implanted within our fabric yet this process is often blocked, repressed and denied in early programming. The discovery process is "like a young child" in expansion, growth and freedom of expression and this quality must be activated, expanded and nurtured from within. TRT within its fabric is "discovery process" opening inner passages to Real Life's deeper meanings. "The door is round and open" to these gateways according to the poem by Rumi, yet you must awaken your Consciousness of the inner planes to find it. **SEE ALSO: AWAKENING, CLARITY, CONSCIOUSNESS, COURAGE, DENIAL, EARS, JOURNAL, JOURNEY, MEDITATION, LEARNING, OBSERVER, UNIVERSAL, UNKNOWN, WHOLE.**

YOUTHFULNESS—Refers to a quality or state of the energy or essence of "youthful" and is *not* limited to the restrictions of chronological age; in higher consciousness, youthfulness refers to qualities of fresh, uplifting, vigorous in spirit, flexible and Light of Heart. TRT allows you to contact, use and expand upon your inner radiance–your inner universal energy which has the energy qualities of radiance, or freshness, of wholeness of involvement, of uplifting spirit and willingness to Be and to participate fully in Life, NO MATTER WHAT! **SEE ALSO: AGING PROCESS, JOY, LAUGHTER, LOVING, RELAXATION, STRESS, YOGA, ZEST.**

AWARENESS/CONSCIOUSNESS–Refers to watchfulness and Consciousness. Your awareness of all planes of existence can be limited or can be in an ongoing process of expanding. TRT accesses the plane of consciousness called "universal transcendent–"The Whole." In using TRT on a regular basis throughout your life you will be on a journey of expanding your Consciousness to 'universal'–on the path of The Great Liberation, on the universal Heart journey. **SEE ALSO: AWAKE, CONSCIOUSNESS, ENERGY, ENLIGHTENMENT, HEART CENTER, INNER PLANE SCIENCE, JOURNAL, JOURNEY, OBSERVER, SOUL, UNIVERSAL, WHOLENESS.**

STRESS–Stress describes daily war and tear on our bodies, emotions, mind and spirit. Stress extended over a period of time without release can drain your energy, sap your vitality and lower your resistance to disease. Stress is also associated with premature aging and chronic debilitating physical conditions. Stress also disturbs your emotional and mental balance. TRT is a complete, unique, self-help technique which promotes the reduction of stress and the balancing of your entire body-emotion-spirit dynamic. In using TRT you will be balancing and restoring your energy, depleted by accumulated stress from the rigors of modern, daily life. In order to de-stress and to promote positive stress responses, you must have a technique which supports your entire dynamic with wholeness. TRT inherently is such a technique. Stress related to jobs and business can be balanced by applying TRT while at work since it can be used conveniently in any situation at any time and requires no extra equipment. **SEE ALSO: BALANCING, BEHAVIOR, BUSINESS, CALMING, CENTERING, JOB, RELAXATION, RELEASE, WHOLENESS, WORK.**

SINGING–TRT is a vibrational energy technique and accesses directly universal, whole energy which can be applied for growth, expansion and alignment of the vibrations of your voice and your vocal energy. Singing is a powerful interaction with the Throat Center, one of the seven major energy centers or chakras. Expanded use of TRT increases the inner radiance of your natural sound, stabilizing your natural power and releasing the full vibrational spectrum of your vocal capacity. Using TRT helps in releasing any restrictions in the flow of your natural sound. **SEE ALSO: BALANCING, ENERGIZE, ENERGY, HEART CENTER, JOY, MUSIC, STRESS, THROAT, THROAT CENTER, VOICE, WHOLE.**

LOVE–Has the aspect of human or brotherly love which is referred to as love of the outer heart–love with an object. This kind of love is the warm feeling of affection felt or sensed from the chest/heart area, love from the lower planes. This kind of love is different from the love known as Divine, Spiritual, Universal, Radiant Love that simply *IS* without external, outer stimulus or object. You can use TRT for expansion of both of these kinds of love and for deeper insights into the vibration of Real Love. **SEE ALSO: COURAGE, EXPANSION, HEART CENTER, MEDITATION, POLARITY, UNIVERSAL LOVE.**

PATTERNS, OF BEHAVIOR–Refers to those behaviors that persons adopt as their own that have actually come from models outside themselves such as from their family or culture. Often these patterns of behavior are hidden beneath the level of awareness and yet are strongly incorporated in every interaction. In using TRT you are beginning a deeper process of awareness with yourself, touching the universal within you and supporting and expanding awareness of the interconnected patterns of your outer planes. Have your awareness journal nearby so that you may have a continuum with your observations of yourself. **SEE ALSO: AWARENESS/CONSCIOUSNESS, BEHAVIOR, CONTINUUM, JOURNAL, MATRIX, MODEL, NATURAL, OBSERVER, REALIZE, UNIVERSAL, WHOLENESS.**

FORGIVING–TRT accesses Universal, whole energy which supports releasing of different kinds of *lower*, not whole, energies whether they are positive or negative. Forgiving is a process of letting go, of releasing. TRT will support this process and the transformation of lower energies to a higher vibration. **SEE ALSO: CHOICE, DISCOVERY PROCESS, EXPANSION, KINDNESS, LOVING, RELEASE, REPRESSION, SILENCE, UNIVERSAL LOVE.**

APPENDIXES

Appendix A

Questions and Answers

The questions included in this section are some of those most frequently asked at public lectures and in TRT Seminars.

What is The Radiance Technique?

TRT is a precise art and science of accessing and amplifying natural, whole, Universal energy and of balancing natural energy by restoring vital energy to all levels of your being. TRT is a vibrational energy science of Universal, Cosmic, Radiant Energy. TRT accesses directly radiant, whole energy and when used as instructed promotes healing, wholeness and wellness, and can be used for attaining higher consciousness and, ultimately, Enlightenment. A self-help technique, TRT is an activator of whole, non-dual, energy from within, a releasor and a transformer of energy from a denser to lighter vibration. TRT is a precise and intact science for balancing and aligning to a higher order of energy (Universal Radiance) your energies within your physical-emotional-mental-spiritual dynamic.

Who Can Learn TRT?

TRT can be taught to virtually anyone. The age range that I have taught is from three to ninety-three years. I have taught TRT to people of high health levels who planned to use TRT for stress reduction, relaxation, and prevention of illness. I have also taught TRT to persons in terminal phases of diseases for relaxation, pain relief, and higher consciousness growth. If for some reason an individual cannot learn TRT, then relatives, friends, and therapists can easily learn to give TRT sessions. Children can also be taught TRT easily and can give the hands-on sessions to a parent or other family member needing help. TRT gives a wonderful way for family members and friends to interact in a nondistressful, relaxing, nondemanding, nonintrusive, peaceful, caring, and loving manner.

Will TRT Interfere with My Personal Religious Beliefs?

No. TRT itself is not a religion or a cult of any kind. It is a harmless and gentle method of activating universal energy within you and using that natural, life-force energy in accordance with your particular needs.

Do I Have to "Believe In" TRT?

No. TRT is not a belief system nor is it a dogma or a doctrine. TRT is a way to access Transcendental, Radiant energy.

Is TRT a Form of Psychic Healing?

No. TRT is a way of activating natural, universal energy and applying it in a specific manner. TRT accesses an order of energy which is transcendental in vibration and is whole, non-dual, harmless energy. Several known psychics have studied TRT with me and found that their psychic powers expanded greatly.

Is TRT an Occult Practice?

The word "occult" unfortunately has taken on certain negative connotations reflective of narrow prejudices in our culture. "Occult" means, literally, "something hidden from view." In tracing some of the history of TRT, I found that this technique was sometimes hidden away and taught only to a chosen, special few, to the elite, and to the aristocracy. TRT is now available to anyone wanting to study it.

Do I Need any Special Knowledge before I Can Take the TRT Seminar?

No. But an openness to learning and growing helps! In the Seminar, you will be thoroughly instructed in the uses of

150

TRT. Included in the courses offered is information on wholistic health and living wholeness, natural healing, and energy balancing. When you have completed the seminar, you will be able to use TRT for yourself and for family or friends if you choose.

Will Use of TRT Interfere with My Medical Prescriptions and Treatments?

No. TRT can easily and successfully be combined with medical therapies and can be used with positive benefits before and after surgery. Many medical doctors have studied TRT and agree that TRT enhances the natural healing process. In addition, TRT can be used in combination with exercise, nutrition, and other techniques and remedies.

How Often Do I Have to Use TRT?

For the most effective benefits from TRT, one needs to use this technique on a daily basis or at least a reasonable amount of time during each week. In the Seminar, you will be given specific directions in the use of TRT according to individual needs.

If I Take the TRT Seminar and Then Do Not Use it, Do I Have to Repeat the Course?

No. Once you have received the TRT activating energy attunements and instructions on applying the technique, you have it for life. The energy does not run out but will amplify with use. I have often received letters from people who did not use TRT for as many as two years after taking the seminar. Those people have been able "to take up where they left off," so to speak, and benefit from using TRT years later.

How Would a Person Not Benefit from Use of TRT?

By *not using* TRT on a regular basis as instructed in the seminar. Too often people are looking for a quick solution to difficulties and diseases that took years to accumulate. TRT is not a "gimmick" or a "quick fix" but is an effective, precise method of amplifying, directing, and using Universal Radiant Energy—but you have to use it to get benefits! When used as instructed, TRT helps you to break up and transform negative habits and patterns into positive, self-renewing ones.

Can TRT Be Effective in Helping to Control Addictive Habits Such as Excessive Smoking, Alcoholic Drinking, and Compulsive Overeating?

Yes. TRT helps you to unblock and release energy that is blocked in your physical, emotional, and mental bodies. TRT promotes release of the underlying distress usually associated with such addictions. TRT can also be easily used *anywhere* for a few minutes instead of smoking a cigarette, taking an alcoholic drink, or eating excessively. Daily use of TRT gives you a direct, easy, safe way of building a habit toward your own positive wellness. TRT is not, however, a substitute for exercise and vital, natural foods, and other appropriate therapies and medical treatments.

Appendix B

Autobiographical Sketch
of the Author

As we journey through our lives, it often happens that we begin to awaken to a sense of ourselves as a whole, unfolding process. We go through cycles, we live through a myriad of events, situations, and relationships, and we even repeat patterns until something happens that changes us, taking us beyond the limits of our past.

Our individual lives differ in the outer context and details. We have different names, different skin tones, different friends, live in different countries, speak different languages, and express ourselves in different ways. Yet in the essence of the life-force energy, we are connected, we are one. From the inside, we are of the same source, and in our hearts, we have a common meeting center of love and, ultimately, light.

I once thought of my life in terms of beginnings and endings. Gradually, I began to perceive of my life as an unfolding process moving along a spiraling continuum. My perspective expanded from seeing events, situations, and relationships as isolated and unrelated to seeing them as interrelated and part of a larger whole. In retrospect, I found that I had often misinterpreted events and that what had once seemed negative often turned out to be positive–perspective transforms everything!

Where did my journey to discovering The Radiance Technique begin? In relating some of the highlights of this process, I will make no attempt to interpret. I have long since learned that interpretations keep one from experiencing "what is." At times, some of the meanderings and some of the twists and turns of my life seemed disjointed, lacking in coherence, and even strange. Surely you know the feeling! By the time I was in high school, I had it all planned. Basically, the scenario was that I would go to college, major in Latin, teach Latin in high school until retirement, marry, have a family, travel, grow old, and die. Are you smiling yet—laughing even? In fact, some of that scenario did happen.

From the very first day of Latin class, I knew I would become a Latin teacher. I will never forget the experience for it had impressed me even more than I had realized at the time. When I opened the Latin book, it was as though closed gates in my memory tracts were thrown suddenly wide open. I knew *that* language! I could read it without knowing how I was doing it. Inwardly, I was experiencing a mixture of amazement, excitement, confusion, and fear. Outwardly, I did what everyone else was doing—listened and learned.

I studied Latin for four years in high school. Each step opened more channels in my memory. I did extra work, reading through text after text as well as studying Roman history. I won a scholarship to study Latin at Florida State University in Tallahassee, Florida. Selected to participate in a special honors program, I received a B.A. and an M.A. in five years, majoring in Latin, Greek, and ancient civilizations with a minor in history. I was elected to Phi Beta Kappa in my junior year. While finishing my master's degree, I met and married another graduate student.

I obtained a teaching position at the internationally known and top-ranked Melbourne High School in Melbourne, Florida. I was hired to teach Latin but instead spent the first semester teaching English literature and humanities. This was one of those twists to which I was referring.

In the late 1960s, I returned to Florida State to work on a doctorate. I had obtained an assistantship to teach Latin. Then came another twist. At the last minute, I was shifted to teaching the mythology course. I resisted but to no avail. You might be thinking that by then I would have caught on to the concept that "life is an unfolding process"—but no, not yet!

Then a startling thing happened. In the three years of teaching mythology, my life was transformed. The research I did in preparation for this class threw open the doors to a new dimension. I discovered that the "myths" of the ancients were filled with vital information and essential *keys* to the meaning and mystery of life. Freud led to Jung, and Jung led to the study of comparative mythology and to Joseph Campbell and endless books and articles, all revealing the same inner messages of these ancient myths which varied only in the outer forms of local names and places. Again and again, the knowledge of life, the essence of existence, and the keys to the "inner secrets" were revealed hidden beneath the outer trappings and the escapades of the local deities. To focus only on the outer was to miss the key to the inner treasure.

It was not unusual to find alterations and modifications of these myths in their outer forms through the centuries, but, in the inner part, the essential truth was transmitted without change. I discovered that these myths connected us to our source directly from the *inside*, providing the knowledge of our cosmic connection and opening the gates of initiation to higher Consciousness. Without this essential information, without this knowledge of who we are and what our essence is, we become lost in the maze of events in what seems like a meaningless, even futile life. When we lose conscious touch with our connection, with our source, we are in the dark and we become afraid.

My own course work included Classics, Near Eastern ancient civilizations, Renaissance history, art history, contemporary art history, and a variety of humanities courses tracing man's intellectual, cultural, and scientific developments into modern times. In March 1970, I received an interdepartmental doctorate degree in humanities. Until 1976, I continued in a career of college teaching.

I had acquired an in-depth and extensive knowledge of where mankind had been from ancient to contemporary times. From 1959 to 1970, I had been constantly in touch with information about our past on this planet. It was not possible to ignore an entire body of knowledge about the so-called mystery schools or ageless wisdoms prevalent for so long in Egypt,

Greece, Rome, and the Near Eastern civilizations. I had also developed an academic interest in the ancient healing arts, which I have continued to pursue through these years.

In 1972, I won a Fulbright Scholarship to study Renaissance and baroque art in Italy at the University of Rome, studying in Florence and Venice. For me, being in Italy was a profound, transforming experience. All the centuries were represented there commingling in an incredibly vibrant dance of modern life. While in Italy, I was able to continue my own study of the inner knowledges and healing arts which had been preserved in myths, religions, and visual, symbolic forms.

When I returned from Italy, I began an extensive investigation of various forms of energy systems and healing arts. I did some study in humanistic and transpersonal psychotherapies and also took astrology courses at Emory University. I studied and taught courses in meditation, parapsychology, and a wide variety of healing arts and sciences including the Tibetan Art and Science of the Mandala. I had become particularly involved in wholistic dimensions in healing, health, and consciousness and in the dawning of this New Age of humanity—the Age of Aquarius.

In 1976, I shifted my full attention to lecturing, private counseling, and working with healing in the area of wholistic health, wholeness, and techniques for achieving higher Consciousness. In addition, I continued my search for healing and energy-balancing methods that would tap universal life-energy in the ways I had known were possible from my formal studies of antiquity.

In 1978, I took the basic course in The Radiance Technique. From my specialized academic background, I was readily able to identify this technique as an ancient method for accessing universal energy and for applying this transcendental energy for balancing, healing, wholing, and enlightening. The origins of this technique are to be found in ancient Egypt and Tibet, perhaps dating more than eight thousand years ago. This knowledge was taken eventually into India, China, and Japan as well as into Greece and Rome. TRT is an ancient art and science of Cosmic, Universal Energy—an inner plane science of Inner Light.

156

In the four years before my discovery of TRT, I had been gaining experience in working as a healer with a number of healing and wholing techniques. In TRT, I recognized the piece missing from those other techniques—the process of accessing, at will regardless of your state of consciousness, a higher order of energy called Transcendental, Radiant Energy. I had never previously encountered a natural energy-balancing and healing method as complete and as effective as TRT. In addition, TRT is for maintaining health and balance as well as for attaining higher Consciousness, spiritual growth, and, ultimately, Enlightenment.

I continued my study of TRT and became an Authorized Instructor. Having found such a remarkable technique, which had been passed in various forms through the centuries, I wanted to be able to teach The Radiance Technique to others. During the last two years of her life, Hawayo Takata taught me the complete system and carefully instructed me in the advanced levels of TRT—all seven degrees. What I learned in this in-depth process enabled me to validate TRT as a Cosmic Science of Light and its ancient origins with additional certainty.

In 1978, I opened a Center in Atlanta, Georgia, and began keeping records of my healing and wholing work with TRT. The extensive experience I obtained from working long hours as a TRT therapist gave me extensive practical experience and knowledge of TRT as a natural cosmic energy art and science. I also gained and continue to gain deep insights and sensitivity to the entire healing, wholing, and personal transformation process. Such knowledge can come only from extensive, direct experiences in working with myself and with many others. In this book, you, the reader, have the combined benefit both of my academic expertise as to what TRT is and of my proficiency and insights obtained from my continuing practice as a user and instructor of TRT.

Ultimately, The Radiance Technique is not words, is not a discussion or a debate, is not a dogma or a doctrine, is not a religion, cult, or belief system, but is a direct, meaningful, and personal accessing of and experience with Universal, Radiant, Light-energy. The information I have shared in this book was intended for a wide range of individuals. If there are chapters and discussions to which you do not relate or have no interest, remember that the words can at best only describe the process and that, in the end, TRT is an *experience*. As Einstein stated, "All knowledge about reality begins with experience and terminates in it."

For me, it is a deep honor to be able to teach others the unique and profound Universal Energy Science of TRT and to work with so many people as a TRT healing/wholing therapist so that we may all achieve our divine birthright: wellness, wholeness, and Enlightenment. Ultimately, use of TRT opens you to profound and personal experiences with Universal, Radiant, Light-energy.

A Note for the New Expanded Edition (1992):

You will notice that this book traces the history of the term 'reiki' and the relationship of the 'reiki' factor in The Radiance Technique®. Author Barbara Ray, known world-wide as the expert and authority on this technique, has brought this historic book, first printed in 1980 as a hard-bound edition, up to date for readers. In the '80s the term reiki was being widely and indiscriminately used to describe any number of unrelated techniques and, consequently, lost its meaning. In this new expanded edition, the original two forewords and the original preface by Dr. Ray are included, and since the term *reiki* was used to reach the readers of that time, it has been left as such. Those materials, and others that follow, have been dated as to their timing and are included for those readers who may be interested.

However, you will note that the text of this "first" book moves into the present and describes this unique system and energy science as The Radiance Technique®, expanding in each chapter the relationship of The Radiance Technique® (TRT) with all the various aspects of life. This edition of the book is exceptional in its clarity and dedication to being informative and unique for each reader.

A SPECIAL READER'S NOTE: Throughout this book you will notice that I sometimes use The Radiance Technique® which includes the correct ® delineating it as a registered service mark. This mark is registered for the use of The Radiance Technique Association International, Inc. and for Authorized Instructors. It denotes this authentic technique and no other. Its use in books such as this is to refer to the actual and authentic technique itself and no others. Sometimes in this book, I have used the words without the registered mark, which is correct to do since it has previously been introduced properly. I have also used TRT to stand for this service-marked phrase.

A Word From the Author
(May 1988)

This book was first published in January 1983, early in the decade of the Eighties when the technique known as 'reiki' was little known to the population of the U.S. and was literally unknown to those in most other countries. In fact, so little was and is known of the use of such transcendental energy sciences, and specifically of this science and system, that a "first book" about 'reiki' was needed to open the doorways for people to being to learn more. Readers were, and still are, particularly interested in what this technique could *do* for them—what kinds of interactions it could have in their own daily lives. For the most part, people wanted to know about the human aspect of using this cosmic science. To meet that need, this book was written primarily for the purpose of making available a gateway to a rich variety of descriptive data reflecting many experiences of people using this technique in their daily lives. In continuing to support this reader interest and benefit, please note that this new expanded edition now *includes* many additional descriptions of uses and personal experiences written by individual students of this cosmic science. Please refer to pages 114-126 for these sharings and experiences.

Since the initial publication of this unique book, thousands of readers have read the earlier editions and have gained an enormous amount of information about Light-energy, sciences of Transcendental, Cosmic energy, about specific uses and applications of this science for personal growth and transformation, for the healing/wholing process within the body-mind-spirit dynamic and about specific ways of interacting with other people as well as with pets, animals and other living energies. So, too, for present and future readers, this special volume, an historical first, will continue to serve well as an invaluable source of information, of insight and of inspiration regarding this unique Universal energy science whether or not they ever go on to a seminar actually to learn the technique itself.

When the first edition of *The Reiki Factor* was published, the word 'reiki' was being used as an adjective, as a verb, as a noun, as the name of the science and as referring to the uses of this technique as well. The book was written in that fashion in order to reach the reader. However, since that time, the word 'reiki' has been used in such generalized and vague ways that new terms are now used to designate this authentic, science and technique. The Radiance Technique® and The Official Reiki Program® now distinguish for the public this authentic, intact science of universal energy and clearly remove the confusion that resulted from the abuse of the word 'reiki' often misapplied randomly to techniques other than the original and authentic science itself. For further information, please refer to "A Special Notice," on page 163 of this edition.

At the time of the first publication of this book, the American-International Reiki Association, Inc., which has since trained and certified a number of instructors worldwide, had just begun the vigorous process of certifying instructors, educating the public, and beginning the process of clarification and of lessening the confusion around the little that was known of 'reiki' as a science of transcendental energy. At that time, there were some historical boundaries that had been set and I continued them in order to work with the information that was then generating through the public and, at that time, to begin to educate readers about what they were most interested in—the uses of the universal energy being called 'reiki'. During the time since the first publication, a cycle of greater education and public interaction has taken place that has proven the wisdom of how this initial outreach to readers was designed.

In selecting the book title, *The Reiki Factor*, I was referencing the *factor* of universal, whole, transcendental Light-energy within each of us and within all living beings, and this radiant, cosmic principle of energy (rei) as a factor interacting with a lower, denser principal of energy (ki) in our daily lives.

My own journey with transcendental energy sciences has been lifelong although I learned this specific technique in 1978. In 1979, I became a 'Reiki' Master, a full Third Degree Initiator, and received complete training in all Seven Degrees of the intact energy science rediscovered by Dr. Mikao Usui in the mid-to-late Nineteenth Century. I founded the Reiki Center in Atlanta in 1978 and, in 1980, the American Reiki Association,

Inc., which soon became the American-International Reiki Association, Inc., and is now The Radiance Technique Association International, Inc.

My academic background and worldwide travel to enhance and to expand my knowledge of Ancient Cultures and Civilizations had prepared me to be able to identify and to explore many inner sciences of transcendental energy. Thus, when I came into contact with this unique science with its precise inner system accessing directly inner universal energy, I was able to identify it properly as such. Since the first publication of this book, I have continued to encourage the collecting and sharing of descriptive experiential data and also have been able to write and to educate others in more detail about the actual science itself. (Please see page 178 for further listing of books and other resources.)

In this first book, I published what was the beginning of important and evolutionary data collecting based on specific experiences of what happens with people who use The Radiance Technique® ('reiki') in their daily lives. This information is a first step into a special kind of social research—one based on ongoing data collecting of a wide variety of experiences with the process of the interaction of inner transcendental energy with other kinds of energy, denser in vibration. I have an intimate, first-hand knowledge of the application of Light-energy and I wrote this book to share some of this special kind of social research with you, the readers.

Although it is simply not possible to teach this science in *any* book form as this transcendental energy science, in particular, requires a living dynamic of interactions in a unique, prescribed and orderly process in order to access, activate and expand inner Universal energy, it is, however, possible for you to gain meaningful, and personally valuable, information for you to have a widely expansive experience in your journey through this book.

Remember, True Healing is a process involving all aspects of your Being and is a celebration of attaining wholeness and oneness—Enlightenment is Your Divine, Cosmic Birthright!

A Special Notice

The Evolution of
The Radiance Technique®

The term rei-ki is from two distinct Japanese words combined by Dr. Usui to denote the cosmic energy science he rediscovered in ancient texts. "Rei" refers to Cosmic, Universal energy and "ki" refers to the life energy of the physical, outer planes. By making the term rei-ki, Dr. Usui merely conveyed in words the concept of the energy of The Whole, the aligning of the part (ki) with the Whole, Universal (Rei) in an ever-expanding principle of dynamic interaction. In choosing the title *The Reiki Factor* for the first book on the science, I used the term 'reiki' to describe this universal factor inherent within this science of transcendental energy. The Radiant power of this science is accessed and transmitted through its inner-connected system of universal symbols and Attunement Processes, *not* through the saying of the word rei-ki or any word at all. The Official Reiki Program®, The Radiance Technique®, Real Reiki®, *is not* a system of words or word limitations. Simply a generic term, rei-ki can be used by anyone for anything. Therefore, Real Reiki®, The Radiance Technique®, The Official Reiki Program®, are registered terms for denoting and distinguishing from "other reiki things" the intact and complete cosmic, vibratory energy science rediscovered by Dr. Usui.

Since *The Reiki Factor* was originally published, the use of this technique has grown in a world-wide outreach that now encircles the globe. During this time, extensive fragmentation

163

and confusion in thinking have occurred concerning the polluted and disconnected "something called reiki" and the actual intact science that was rediscovered by Dr. Usui. Individuals who do not have access to the whole system and who do not even have knowledge of the correct Attunement Processes have been randomly "making teachers." Using parts disconnected from the whole system and making up formulas and methods which were never related to the activation of the energy of this system is a process that has NO RELATION WHATEVER TO THIS SYSTEM REDISCOVERED BY DR. USUI. It is "something" other than this science. And those individuals have none of the ingredients necessary for the orderly process of this science to occur. WHATEVER THAT "SOMETHING" IS, THEY HAVE CALLED IT "reiki."

To denote the difference, the intact science has been called "The Official Reiki Program®" and an even clearer denotation has been added from the polluted "something" that is called "reiki," that of "The Radiance Technique®." That which is being called "reiki" right now is NOT the system that Dr. Usui rediscovered. The Official Reiki Program®, The Radiance Technique®, "Real Reiki®, *IS* that system and The Radiance Technique Association International, Inc. (T.R.T.A.I.) guarantees that it is that intact system.

The Radiance Technique®; The First Degree, The Second Degree or The Third Degree Official Reiki Programs®; and Real Reiki® are NOT synonyms for "reiki." The word "reiki" is *not* the same as any of these terms and the word "reiki" is NOT interchangeable with these terms. Legally, no one who has not been certified and trained as an Authorized Instructor can use these registered service marks.

Before spending your energy, your time, and your money, be sure that you will be studying the intact science rediscovered by Dr. Usui. Contact the T.R.T.A.I.

Two additional books on the authentic Usui system have been written which are available to you. *The Official Handbook of The Radiance Technique®* is a new and completely expanded edition that has important information and exercises for using the technique for students of all Degrees of study. It contains two full-color photographs and a beautiful design for easy study and discovery when applying The Radiance Technique®. It offers you opportunities for expansion and exploration for your own personal advancement in consciousness, growth, and transformation.

The Expanded Reference Manual is truly the first of its kind with a unique "A to Z" design for study and *over 600 entries*! You can deepen your knowledge of the multi-dimensional relationships of The Radiance Technique® with the outer planes of everyday life and the inner planes of higher consciousness. Designed for students and alumni of every Degree of study, the references offer guidance for applying radiant energy to deepen your interrelationship to the inner plane energies of all living systems. Cross references lead your journey of discovery and your celebration of Light and the joys of awakening and awareness.

Much of the information in *The Expanded Reference Manual* would be valuable and beneficial to people in their personal growth and transformation on the Path of Awakening, even if they have not yet studied The Radiance Technique®, The Official Reiki Program®, which cannot be learned from *any* book. To learn this technique you will need to be taught by a fully qualified and currently Authorized Instructor. However, *The Expanded Reference Manual* is so comprehensive that serious students of consciousness will be using it for centuries to come.

Information on resources for these books and for other information is on the Addresses page.
(1987)

Foreword

to First Edition of *The Reiki Factor*

It is a privilege to give my enthusiastic endorsement to the public presentation of Reiki Healing. In 1979 my husband[1] and I were fortunate to meet Dr. Barbara Ray and learn about this significant healing method. Since then we have developed much personal appreciation of the healing power of Reiki.

In March 1979, my husband had surgery for stomach cancer; it had spread to the adjacent lymph nodes. Eight months later the incision had not healed despite repeated surgical interventions. At that time we attended a lecture on Reiki Healing by Dr. Ray and we decided that John should avail himself of such treatments. Seventeen days later his incision was entirely healed. He has had no further symptoms of cancer.

We now have both attained The First and The Second Degree in the Reiki Method of Natural Healing.

My mother had surgery for cancer of the colon in August 1979, at eighty-five years of age. There was lymph node involvement. Mother got her First Degree in Reiki and utilized it on herself. Through eighteen months of chemotherapy she had no hair loss and no weight loss, and her energy level remained high. We believe that her daily hour of self-administered Reiki treatments was a significant factor in her unexpectedly good recovery. Her cancer has not recurred.

---

[1]John Warkentin, Ph.D., M.D.

Reiki Healing also helped my mother with the stress of my father's illness during the last months of their sixty years together. In January 1980, my father entered a nursing home because of the recurrence of hydrocephalus, for which he had had surgery the preceding January. He received many Reiki treatments during the ensuing two and one-half years and always felt calmed after them. I believe Reiki contributed much to his well-being in the final months and helped him to make his transition peacefully.

In my own person I have repeatedly experienced the healing power of Reiki energy. Although I have not had a life-threatening illness in recent years, the stress from these past three and one-half years led to lesser illnesses and pains of various origins. These were significantly relieved or healed primarily by means of Reiki. A particular experience was when I had a very painful fall, landing heavily on my left knee. It began swelling rapidly so that the entire knee was conspicuously larger, with a special anterior protrusion the size of a large egg. Within an hour I got to the Atlanta Reiki Center where I was treated for two hours. The swelling decreased and the anterior protrusion was gone. That evening I was treated for an hour by four Reiki healers simultaneously; after that the swelling had entirely subsided. A physician who saw the knee swell immediately after I fell expected me to be on crutches for at least several days. He was amazed that same evening to see me walking with little pain and no swelling of the injured knee.

Two and one-half days ago I sprained my right ankle. My husband and I Reiki-ed it periodically for several hours and put on an Ace bandage. I could not walk without crutches, and the following morning I saw an orthopedist who found no fracture but diagnosed a severe sprain. He was very surprised at the absence of swelling in my foot and ankle. He said my ankle would have to be bandaged for two or three weeks and I would have to walk with crutches or a cane and be unable to drive for at least a week. With the help of Reiki there was never any swelling, and, today, forty-eight hours later, I am able to walk without help and am driving my car.

The foregoing personal vignettes indicate some of my experience with the effectiveness of Reiki healing. The great variety of human diseases that can be favorably influenced or healed by the Reiki Method is very surprising and, at times, has seemed miraculous. The Reiki modality appears to operate via energy that is present around us at all times. I do not understand the precise nature of this energy. I do not know the mechanism by which the energy involved has a beneficent effect rather than a harmful one. Quite regularly pain is relieved rather than made worse; physical and emotional healing is promoted rather than hindered as a result of Reiki intervention. I do not know the limitations of Reiki healing. I am particularly mystified by the evidences of effective absentee Reiki healing, where healer and patient are separated by many miles. Finally, since this healing energy is apparently universally present, how can we understand the neglect by humankind of such a great good?

In the face of so many questions, I have only one clear response: whatever the mechanism, Reiki healing works!

I admire the courage of Dr. Ray in publishing *The Reiki Factor*. She is one of the first American masters of this method and presents a detailed statement of the present knowledge about Reiki. With integrity and dedication she is striving to make Reiki Healing widely available.

July 1982   Elizabeth Valerius Warkentin, Ph.D.

Foreword

to Second Edition of *The Reiki Factor*

I am honored to be asked again to write this Foreword to the second edition of *The Reiki Factor*.

In August 1982, I was privileged to receive The Third Degree as a Master/Teacher of the Reiki Method of Natural Healing. This came at an opportune time. Three months later, in November, my husband was found surgically to have multiple metastatic carcinoma. He was given one to two months to live;

he lived 12 more months. (Medical statistics had given him maximally 1 ½ years to live after his first surgery for a different cancer four years earlier.) In December, while still in the hospital, John received The Third Degree as a Reiki Master/Teacher. I believe that our being initiated as Reiki Masters helped us live through the ensuing year with a lightness that would not otherwise have been present. In addition, I believe I would have completed that following year with a bitterness and cynicism that had started within myself and which began to turn with that initiation.

From the time of his surgery, John was frequently very tired and had daily Reiki treatments from loving people in Atlanta and also absentee Reiki from people throughout the country. He also had four hours of Reiki every Saturday with two to 15 Reiki practitioners. Although he usually started these treatments feeling very tired, when they were over he often said: "That's a miracle; I feel wonderful and full of energy now." His color, too, changed from ashen-grey to healthy-looking pink!

John had had radiation therapy to shrink a tumor in his stomach, but it did not affect the metastases. He was also given a trial of chemotherapy which was unsuccessful for his type of cancer. Despite expectations, he was able to see patients again in May and it gave him great pleasure to be useful to others once more. In late September we saw a cancer specialist in Chicago who told us: "Reiki must be a wonderful thing to enable John to have the energy to make this trip and to have the energy he has for the degree of disease he evidences." John was able to work until the end of October when he became too weak to continue. Medically he was expected to be in a great deal of pain, but he was not. The only medication he took toward the end of his life was for nausea. In addition, after one blood transfusion in March, his blood counts remained well within normal ranges.

It was not only the physical plane on which John was touched by the Reiki. His dying was a process which involved his physical body and also his spiritual self. The healing which took place with the Reiki included that which appears to occur beyond the physical plane. At one time John appeared to be drowning in the fluid in his lungs. I sat next to him hearing the gurgles in his chest. I was in pain with him; he was my husband whom I loved. A friend, who is also a Reiki teacher,[2] came into our bedroom and started to Reiki John. She said to him: "It's beautiful, isn't it?" He opened his eyes, looked directly at her and said: "Yes!" It was as though he were telling us that over and above the physical and psychological torment we saw, he was experiencing incredible beauty. He also said: "I want to live with the Reiki forever." I was in bed with pneumonia next to John at that time. In fact, I had had pneumonia and other respiratory problems a number of times during the past stressful six years. I believe that without Reiki I would not have been able to physically or psychologically withstand the stress of those times.

John was lucid at the time of his transition. He lived his three score and ten years with love and dedication. His devotion was to God and to serving mankind. We both believe the Reiki helped his final years to be relatively pain-free and richly of service. When he made his transition, he stepped out in Light on our 12th wedding anniversary, November 27, 1983. I learned through my husband's dying process that what matters is that you leave this world in light and love of God.

I especially appreciate Dr. Ray for her continued help and service to us during John's final time on this earth. Her dedication to the Reiki and to sharing it with us and with all humankind is reflected in her teachings and in *The Reiki Factor*.

January 1985   Elizabeth Valerius Warkentin, Ph.D.
                        Psychotherapist and Adjunct Professor
                            of Psychology,
                        Georgia State University
                        Reiki Master/Teacher, Atlanta, Georgia

---

[2]Sara Schmidlin, Ph.D.

Preface

This book is a landmark. It is the first book published about Reiki! The word "Reiki" means universal life-force energy. Reiki is a wonderful, unique, profound, and safe technique for activating and amplifying the natural life-force energy within you and for applying this energy to yourself using a precise and scientific method.

Reiki is a powerful yet gentle, subtle yet precise art and science of restoring your depleted energy and of balancing natural energy within you to promote healing, positive wellness, wholeness, higher consciousness, and, ultimately, Enlightenment.

Reiki is not a religion, it is not a dogma, it is not a doctrine, and it is not a cult. Reiki is not a "laying-on-of-hands"—a term that is used in a religious context and is a form of healing involving a strong degree of belief in a particular religion. Rciki is not a belief system nor is it a form of mind control, hypnosis, or wishful thinking.

What, then, is Reiki? It is a natural energy-activating method. It is a precise way of using "Light-energy" to restore and balance your own vital energy—physically, emotionally and mentally—and to connect with your inner self—your spirit. This book puts you in touch with the essence of Reiki. This book is also about Reiki, which means that it contains descriptions. It cannot contain the experience itself. By clearly and directly getting to what the essence of Reiki is and by including discussions of many people's experiences with Reiki, I have hoped to facilitate your understanding of it.

Reiki is easy to learn, completely safe, and requires no special knowledge or additional equipment. You can learn to use

171

Reiki in almost any situation or location, at any time of day that is suitable for your own personal needs. There is no need to alter your consciousness while you are using Reiki. Reiki can be applied effectively on a daily basis to such ailments as headaches, eye strain, physical tensions, and fatigue, as well as to emotional-mental responses such as anxiety, depression, fear, "uptightness," and anger. Reiki can also be used to heal and whole chronic ailments and as a life-force support system in terminal situations. And for those moving in that direction, Reiki is a precise, subtle tool for personal transformation, higher Consciousness, and enlightenment.

Reiki, however, is not used just for when you are sick. It is one of the best ways available for restoring your vital energy, for maintaining your positive wellness, and for preventing disorders. "Positive wellness" refers to a state of health, well-being and wholeness that is not simply the lack of symptoms but reflects a high level of vitality, which is naturally your birthright.

Who can learn Reiki? Virtually anyone of any age is capable of learning this precise, natural, energy-balancing technique. The basic requirement is that you have to be ALIVE on this plane of existence. I have taught Reiki successfully to people from ages five to ninety-three. I have taught Reiki to those who were healthy and to those who were in varying degrees of ill health, including those in terminal states. I have also taught Reiki to blind people and to those with severe physical, emotional, and mental deficiencies.

Who needs Reiki? *You* do—if you are alive and using energy *in any way* each day. Reiki is for the sick and tired who are sick and tired of being sick and tired! And Reiki is for all of you who are healthy and whole and plan to stay that way—no matter what your age!

I have titled this book *The Reiki Factor* to reflect the deep significance to each of us in our lives of the rediscovery and availability now of this wonderful, profound, ancient technique for activating the Light-energy within us and for restoring and balancing our vital energy. Many who have attended my lectures and the Reiki seminars have asked, "Is there a book about Reiki?" and "When are you going to write about Reiki?" No, until this time there was no book about Reiki. Now there is.

The primary purpose of the book is to discuss Reiki, to make it known to you, and to demonstrate the uses and benefits of Reiki in your daily life. A secondary purpose is to put Reiki in the modern context of the "so-called" New Age into which we are now evolving and to relate it to what is called a "wholistic model."

The book is designed so that you may read the chapters in any order you wish, skipping around to those of special interest to you, or read in a linear manner from beginning to end. But to assure yourself a full comprehension and deeper understanding of Reiki, please read the whole book.

Many who have already taken the Reiki seminars have called it the "gift of the universe" and "the precious gift of life." Again and again I am told, "Reiki is the best investment I have ever made in my *life*," and "I don't know how anyone lives without Reiki!"

In the end, Reiki is not words, it is not an intellectual debate, and it is not an emotional panacea. Reiki is a unique, individual *experience* of using natural energy in a specific way to promote balanced energy, healing, wholeness, and positive wellness in your being and in your life no matter who you are, where you are, or what your age. When Reiki is used *as instructed* on a regular basis in your life, you will be participating consciously and directly in the process of restoring your vital energy, of healing, of gaining wholeness, and of promoting higher consciousness and enlightenment of yourself according to *your own natural process*.

It is an honor to share Reiki with each of you in the form of this book. It is a privilege to have the opportunity to give public lectures and to instruct you in this incredibly gentle art and precise science of Reiki. I invite each of you to read the book, to take a Reiki seminar, and to open the Reiki experience directly to yourself. Meanwhile, enjoy the book, learn, grow, and be well.

Barbara Ray

Atlanta, Georgia
January 1982

Acknowledgments

There are no words adequate to express my deep gratitude for *all* who have supported and contributed time and effort to the Reiki Center in Atlanta, Georgia, and to the founding and success of the American-International Reiki Association, Inc., now known as The Radiance Technique Association International, Inc.

Special thanks are given to the hundreds of persons who have given accounts of the profound benefits they have received from using The Radiance Technique®. They will recognize their contributions throughout this book.

For his support of my work in wholistic health, and the certification program for Authorized Instructors, many thanks go to Terry S. Friedmann, M.D., director of Holistic Medical Clinic in Venice, Florida, and one of the founders of the American Holistic Medical Association.

Thanks to Fred W. Wright, Jr., writer-journalist, and Marvelle Lightfields, writer-teacher-counselor, for reading and commenting upon sections of the manuscript, and to Yesnie Carrington and my mother, Jean Jack, for their constant support, humor, and long hours of "rough-draft" typing of the manuscript.

A special expression of gratitude is given for the enduring support and encouragement of my dear friends, the doctors, the psychotherapists, and other health-care professionals who have endorsed this radiant technique, this book, and my work in healing and wholing.

Eternal gratitude is given to the late Hawayo Takata for a deep friendship and full training in this ancient cosmic science and to Dr. Mikao Usui who rediscovered this profound technique.

And, last but not least, many thanks to both of my parents for giving me the opportunity to be here now working and serving in this New Age of Humanity. (1980)

Notes

1. INTRODUCTION: A NEW BEGINNING

1. William Morris (ed.), *The American Heritage Dictionary of the English Language* (Boston: Houghton Mifflin Co., 1980), p. 908.

2. Lincoln Barnett, *The Universe and Dr. Einstein* (New York; A Bantam Book, 1969), p. 108.

2. DAWNING OF A "NEW AGE" OF CONSCIOUSNESS AND THE RADIANCE TECHNIQUE®

1. Alvin Toffler, *The Third Wave* (New York: Bantam Books, Inc., 1981), p. 9.

2. Ibid.

3. THE WHOLISTIC MODEL

1. Harold Bloomfield and Robert Kory, *The Holistic Way to Health and Happiness* (New York: Simon and Schuster, 1978), p. 23.

2. Marilyn Ferguson, *The Aquarian Conspiracy* (Los Angeles: J. P. Tarcher, 1980), p. 85.

6. UNIVERSAL ENERGY AND THE RADIANCE TECHNIQUE®

1. Jean Charon, "The Spirit: In Man . . . In Contemporary Physics" at the Second World Congress of Science and Religion, St. Petersburg Beach, Florida, June 1981.

2. Jolande Jacobi (ed.), *C. G. Jung: Psychological Reflections—a New Anthology of His Writings, 1095-1961* (Princeton: Princeton University Press, 1978), p. 30 and p. 36.

3. Quoted by Roland Gammon in the paper "Scientific Mysticism" at the Second World Congress of Science and Religion, St. Petersburg Beach, Florida, June 1981.

4. Quoted by Kay Croissant and Catherine Dees in *Continuum—the Immortality Principle* (San Bernardino: Franklin Press, 1978), p. 35.

7. THE RADIANCE TECHNIQUE®: A SCIENCE OF TRANSCENDENTAL LIGHT ENERGY

1. Ferguson, *The Aquarian Conspiracy*, p. 102.

2. Ibid., p. 32.

3. John Ott, *Health and Light* (New York: Pocket Books, 1976), p. 19.

4. Ibid., p. 192.

5. Ibid., p. 21.

6. Albert Einstein and Leopold Infeld, *The Evolution of Physics* (New York: Simon and Schuster, 1938), p. 31.

7. Carl Sagan, *Cosmos* (New York: Random House, 1980), p. 345.

10. STRESS, RELAXATION, AND THE RADIANCE TECHNIQUE®

1. Hans Selye, *Stress Without Distress* (New York: Signet, 1975), p. 14.

2. Simonton, Carl, *Getting Well Again* (New York: Bantam Books, 1978), p. 44.

3. Quoted by Steven Halpern in *Tuning the Human Instrument* (Belmont: Spectrum Research Institute, 1978), p. 53.

4. Simonton, *Getting Well Again*, p. 41.

5. Halpern, *Tuning the Human Instrument*, p. 49.

6. Bloomfield, *The Wholistic Way to Health and Happiness*, p. 50.

13. DYING, DEATH, AND THE RADIANCE TECHNIQUE®

1. Jacobi, *C.G. Jung: Psychological Reflections*, p. 28.

2. Croissant, *Continuum—the Immortality Principle*, p. 7.

3. Ibid., p. 1.

4. Ibid., p. 21.

5. Ibid., p. 23.
6. Ibid., p. 35.
7. Ibid.
8. Ibid., p. 71.
9. Elisabeth Kubler-Ross, *Death–the Final Stage of Growth*, (Englewood Cliffs: Prentice-Hall, Inc. 1975), p. 6.

14. INSTANTANEOUS HEALING WITH THE RADIANCE TECHNIQUE®

1. Quoted by Ferguson in *The Aquarian Conspiracy*, p. 174.
2. Morris (ed.), *The American Heritage Dictionary of the English Language*, p. 680.
3. Ibid., p. 1248.

Selected Bibliography

Barnett, Lincoln. *The Universe and Dr. Einstein*. New York: Bantam Books, 1969.

Beasley, Victor. *Your Electro-Vibratory Body*. Boulder Creek, Calif.: University of the Trees Press, 1978.

Bloomfield, Harold, and Kory, Robert. *The Holistic Way to Health and Happiness*. New York: Simon & Schuster, 1978.

Brenner, Paul. *Health Is a Question of Balance*. New York: Vantage Press, 1978.

Capra, Fritjof. *The Tao of Physics*. New York: Bantam Books, 1977.

Dossey, Larry. *Space, Time & Medicine*. Boulder: Shambhala Publications, Inc., 1982.

Ferguson, Marilyn. *The Aquarian Conspiracy*. Los Angeles: J.P. Tarcher, 1980.

Hall, Manly. *Freemasonry of the Ancient Egyptians*. Los Angeles: Philosophical Research Society, Inc., 1980.

Halpern, Steven. *Tuning the Human Instrument*. Belmont, Calif.: Spectrum Research Institute, 1978.

Kaslof, Leslie. *Wholistic Dimensions in Healing: A Resource Guide*. New York: Doubleday & Co., Inc., 1978.

Keyes, Ken. *Handbook to Higher Consciousness*. St. Mary, Kentucky: Living Love Publications, 1975.

Kubler-Ross, Elisabeth. *On Death and Dying*. New York: Macmillan Publishing Co., Inc., 1970.

——————, *Death-The Final Stage of Growth*. Englewood Cliffs: Prentice-Hall, Inc., 1975.

Montagu, Ashley. *Growing Young*. New York: McGraw-Hill, 1981.

Motoyama, Hiroshi. *Science and the Evolution of Consciousness*. Brookline, Mass.: Autumn Press, Inc., 1978.

Ott, John. *Health and Light*. New York: Pocket Books, 1976.

Sagan, Carl. *Cosmos*. New York: Random House, 1980.

Selye, Hans. *Stress without Distress*. New York: Signet, 1975.

Sheehy, Gail. *Pathfinders*. New York: William Morrow and Co., Inc., 1981.

Simonton, Carl and Simonton, Stephanie. *Getting Well Again*. New York: Bantam Books, 1978.

Swami Rama. *A Practical Guide to Holistic Health*. Honesdale, Penn.: Himalayan International Institute, 1978.

Teilhard de Chardin, Pierre. *Toward the Future*. Translated by Rene Hague. New York: William Collins Sons & Co., Ltd., and Harcourt Brace Jovanovich, Inc., 1975.

Talbot, Michael. *Mysticism and the New Physics*. New York: Bantam Books, 1981.

Wolf, Fred. *Taking the Quantum Leap*. New York: Harper & Row, 1981.

Zukav, Gary. *The Dancing Wu Li Masters: An Overview of the New Physics*. New York: Bantam Books, 1980.

ADDRESSES FOR MORE INFORMATION

For information on The First and The Second Degree seminars and Authorized Instructors in your area;

For information concerning membership in The Radiance Technique Association International, Inc. (T.R.T.A.I.), a non-profit organization;

For sending sharings to or inquiries about "The Radiance Technique Journal";

For information on the book: *The Radiant Performer: The Spiral Path to Performing Power*, by Wesley Balk, Ph.D., University of Minnesota Press:

For information on any books or pamphlets published on The Radiance Technique® to:

The Radiance Technique Association International, Inc.
P.O. Box 40570
St. Petersburg, Florida 33743-0570

For information on these books:
The 'Reiki' Factor in The Radiance Technique®, by Barbara Ray, Ph.D.
The Expanded Reference Manual of The Radiance Technique®, by Barbara Ray, Ph.D.
The Official Handbook of The Radiance Technique®, by Barbara Ray, Ph.D.
The Radiance Technique® On The Job, by Fred W. Wright Jr.
The Radiance Technique® and the Animal Kingdom, by Marvelle Lightfields

Write to the T.R.T.A.I. address above or to:

*Radiance Associates
P.O. Box 86425
St. Petersburg, Florida 33738

*Use this address also to inquire about future publications concerning The Radiance Technique®. New articles, books, and pamphlets with information about TRT are currently being published. Ask for a complete list of publications.

For information on all seminars for The Third Degree and beyond:

Coordinator
Radiance Stress Management International, Inc.
P.O. Box 86425
St. Petersburg, Florida 33738